Tchaikovsky

Unlocking the Masters Series, No. 10

Series Editor: Robert Levine

Tchaikovsky

A Listener's Guide

Daniel Felsenfeld

ab

AMADEUS
PRESS

Published in 2006 by Amadeus Press
512 Newark Pompton Turnpike
Pompton Plains, New Jersey 07444

Printed in the United States of America

Book design by Snow Creative Services

Library of Congress Cataloging-in-Publication Data is available upon request.
ISBN 1-57467-134-0

For quotation of passages from *Tchaikovsky: A Self-Portrait*, compiled by Alexandra Orlova and translated by R. M. Davison, gratitude is expressed to Oxford University Press.

While every effort has been made to trace copyright holders and obtain permission, this has not been possible in all cases; any omissions brought to our attention will be remedied in future editions.

www.amadeuspress.com

For my parents, who gave me space and means to do my work...

...and to Elizabeth, for just about everything

Contents

Acknowledgments

As no book is ever written by a single soul (despite my name alone on the title page), there are, as always, many to thank. For moral support, encouragement, food, food for thought, a nice place to work, a good laugh at the end of the hard days, I would like to thank the friends: Stephanie Wright, Stacy Frierson, Stephanie Mortimore, Marie Mascari, Chris Milenkevich and Randy Hartwell, Tara Bray Smith, Lara Pelegrenelli, Ernie Hilbert, Mark Adamo and John Corigliano, Sherry Gordon, Renee Youn, Rebecca Davis, Michelle Bohlman, Ben Finane, Jeff Buddle and Elaine Perlov, Evan Machlan, Sarah Bynum, Susan Del Giorno, Cary Rosko, Serena McKinney, Paola Prestini, Suzanne Ryan, Tobias Picker, and so many more.

Thanks to the New York Public Library, the coffee shop Half (including Sarah, who served up caffeinated inspiration), and various other places to which I dragged my little laptop for all these months. Thanks also to Mark Berry at Naxos for help getting all the recordings expediently.

To the people at Amadeus Press—John Cerullo and Caroline Howell—thanks again for all your hard work not just on my behalf, but in helping to spread the message about this amazing music. To Dave Hurwitz and Tom May, the other authors of books in this series, you set the bar impossibly high; I hope I can rate. To Robert Levine, heaven's editor, thanks for vision, for help, and mostly for undue patience.

Above all I would like to thank the people to whom I dedicate this book: my parents, Alan and Shirley Felsenfeld, for giving me space and means to go prophet; and Elizabeth Gold, for everything.

And thanks to all of you, for listening . . .

Introduction

Richard Strauss, the emblematic *fin de siècle* musician, believed that in order to be a composer, one had to harbor the desire to oversee a world of beauty—not an inspired calling from on high but an aesthetic reaction to one's own insufferable circumstances. If you are a composer, your music is the one thing in this world you can control absolutely. This desire—to be the CEO of one's own musical destiny—never burned brighter than in Pyotr Ilyich Tchaikovsky. He lived from 1840 to 1893, the time we refer to as the Victorian era, not famous for its moral abandon. He was an erudite, cultured Muscovite, one who kept a ruinous secret. His work, like that of all great artists, is best examined on both a micro and macro level, for the whole of his oeuvre is greater than the sum of his parts.

Welcome, readers, to the Tchaikovsky-verse.

It is a place full of fantastical characters, wild obsessions, an endless supply of gorgeous melodies (and inner melodies), and enough weird experiments to fill ten books of this exact sort. He died in turmoil, but left us the keys to his kingdom in the form of his music. There are common tricks, scraps of craft, means of communication, but on the whole it is a place where beauty triumphs, sadness overwhelms, fancy flourishes, and delight is palpable and defiant, not condemned to margins. To be Russian, possessed of a true Slavic soul, is to suffer—think Chekhov, Dostoyevsky—and the Tchaikovsky-verse certainly does not lack for suffering, especially in the grandeur of the symphonies. But there's more to it than that. There is the twee delight of *Nutcracker,* the bold, elegiac beauty of the Serenade for Strings, the puckish dash of the Violin Concerto, and the overt heart-on-sleeve anguish of the *Romeo and Juliet* Overture. Like the complete work of Tchaikovsky's beloved Shakespeare, this is a world teeming with life, breathing heavily under the weight of its own multidimensional outcry, a vast and complicated landscape akin, also, to another of Tchaikovsky's loves, the poet Dante. Like the Italian's work, there's redemption, fear, anguish, and wandering; like the Englishman's, there's breadth, humor, and the vicissitudes of the human condition. But working in tones, less direct than words, Tchaikovsky is able to live in the abstract, the cracks between this and that realm, to lay out the beauty and terror of the world in a more visceral, less direct way.

This is not a biography. This is not even an attempted biography. This is a book about the music, not the man. There will be details of his life as needed, but only as they pertain to his work. There will be no "this-then-this" retelling of the great man's days, no tracking of events, no essays about his more controversial aspects: his homosexuality, the culture which forbade his homosexuality, his suicide ("did he or didn't he?"). This book is entirely about his music. It is meant for those who want to know more about his work, who are willing to go a little deeper (but who do not want to take the time to do all the back-learning). What this small volume aims at is a discussion of the work in a non-threatening but non-condescending way for the interested but potentially uninitiated listener—this is by no means "Tchaikovsky for Dummies," because if you are reading and therefore interested in knowing more about this music, the last thing you are is a dummy. The hope is that, through exploration of the familiar—you may not know it yet, but you have heard most of the music on the two enclosed discs—you will not just gain insight into the work of this one composer, but feel more at home with classical music in general. Your work is to listen; my task is to give you the tools to do so.

Many friends of mine—other composers, mostly—have, when discovering I was writing a book about Tchaikovsky, questioned my choice. I made impassioned pleas on behalf of the little Russian, but most remained unpersuaded. In school his music was barely discussed, or if it came up at all, it was usually with a grimace. It always seemed that most thought him a cloying melodist, a composer without edge, without substance, outré from the get-go and the creator of unbearably charming music. So why listen? The twentieth century taught us that art had to be hard, reveal ugly truths, speak mostly to the most murderous parts of our nature. It also taught us a notion of progressive lineage, one in which Tchaikovsky (along with Brahms and Dvořák) did not figure. So why pursue an entire book that seeks not to explain the man (though his story is captivating, the stuff of movies and scintillating Proust-level gossip speculation) or his music, but *how one might go about listening to it?* The only answer I have ever been able to come up with—for myself, or for the curious parties—is that his music is just plain good. The more I listened, the more I got, the more I came to love, and the more I wanted to share his tricks, to unveil his secrets, to help others unlock the mysteries.

This book is one quarter as long as it ought to be; there are glaring omissions. Saddest of all, there is no vocal music included. I chose instead to focus on the works by which we know him best, all of which are orchestral. In Tchaikovsky's day, however, he was known primarily as an opera composer, while now his operas, though performed, do not feature in as many seasons at major companies as do the works of Puccini, Wagner, Verdi, or Mozart. I do believe that once you enter the Tchaikovksy-verse for this long and this deeply (however slight the *number* of works discussed), you will never want to leave. I view this book not as an end, but as a portal. You can now go and discover his operas—*Pique Dame, Mazeppa,* and *Eugene Onegin* to name only three—his other symphonies, his chamber music, his songs, his piano pieces . . . and his life story as told in his vast landscape of notes.

It is my hope that you leave this book not merely with a newer understanding of this composer's work, but confident in your set of tools for understanding all music. Giving a work—any work—pride of place in your thoughts more than once will lead you not only to experience the initial shock of the beauty of good music, but the larger satoris that come with getting deep into the matter. Most exciting is that, neophyte or not, you have so many amazing musical scenes ahead of you. Now that you understand a little more about how they might come together and how you might change your paradigm in order to perceive them more clearly, you will not be just their observer—you will be able to actively participate in them.

The idea that listening to music—any music—is an engaged "activity" like reading or movie-going to which one devotes one's entire mind is all but lost. It is therefore critical to know that, at the time when these works were written, this sort of careful listening was expected from the concert audience. To them, themes and modulations were like characters we find in stories. Today, a common criticism of a film or television show is that the characters are simply not believable. In Victorian-era Moscow the same invective might have been leveled at a sonata-allegro movement in a symphony. Since the composer wrote to this sort of attention, it stands to reason that, in order to understand the work—to really *hear* it—you need to listen as his audience did. It is not difficult or time consuming, there's no homework, no written tests, no cocktail-party pop quizzes. All you need is an open set of ears and a desire to get to the heart of the work.

People tend to be frightened of classical music, and who can blame them? It is an intimidating field, partly for the sheer volume of material it encompasses (some nine hundred years and still going strong), partly (sadly) because of some of the judgmental souls who love it. Many people in the milieu use knowledge as a weapon, making it an unwelcoming, closed field. One trip to a high-toned place like the Metropolitan Opera is enough to intimidate; a trip to the local Tower Records can be downright frightening. After all, if you are seeking a boxed set of Beethoven symphonies, do you have any idea which of the sixty (or so) that are currently available you will choose? Turning to those who write about classical music in the press does not help, because the bulk of the critics, with their agendas, their prejudices, and snobbery, tend not to guide but to do the opposite, to push their readers further from the beauty found in the material. Many of the books written *about* music—especially those emblazoned with a ". . . for beginners," or, worse, ". . . for dummies" subheading—are valuable, but a degrading read, hardly volumes to sit honorably on one's bookshelf, doing little in the way of respecting their audience. So how does one sort through the morass to find the million kernels of beauty? There's no easy answer, but a book like this can certainly help.

How to Listen

Listening to classical music is like reading a mystery novel. You need to be involved, attentive, receptive, but the best works (be they symphonies or mysteries) reward this attention. A whodunit has a conceit, a murder that takes place amongst an enclosed cast of characters in a finite location. Trying to concoct a mystery devoid of these prefabrications would result in a dull tale. In order for the form to be as engaging as it can be, these rules must be followed—though, of course, the best writers can bend them slightly, even break them, but only because they are hyper-aware of how they work. The same is true of classical music, although instead of a conceit it has a *form,* the characters are *themes*, and the finite location is the expectation the form allows (the word *symphony* is an excellent example). And as for murder, that is often found in the one thing that pricks your ears at the beginning, a slight bend in the progress, an unpredictable note in the melody, a rhythm you cannot quite square. This does violence to our expectations, and in this violence, glorious music is often born.

One reads a mystery to try to second-guess it, to see if you are quicker on your feet than the fictional detective—and how often are you, really? The same is true of listening to music: instead of allowing sound to *wash over you* (this has to be the ultimate hackneyed cliché of critics), why not see if you can hazard guesses as to what will come next. A poorly written mystery would introduce, in the end, a completely foreign character as the murderer: imagine Agatha Christie's Inspector Poirot or Miss Marple announcing to the anxious room that the butler *whom we have never met* did it? This would disappoint. The same line of thinking holds in a tightly wrought composition: after a certain point, nothing *new* happens, but what *develops* out of what we already know is, in the best music, always surprising.

It is important to know that there are many different ways to listen effectively (and effective—as opposed to "right"—listening, is our aim). Each is suited to the type of music, the intentions of the composer or the work, the individual listener and his or her level of experience, and even the place where one is actually sitting while listening. It would be unwise to listen to a four-hour Wagner opera at the Vienna

Staatsoper in the same way as one might a three-minute song by Debussy at a conservatory student's graduate recital. Mozart's serenades are for a different audience than his symphonies, and the Beethoven of the late quartets requires a certain kind of attention that the Beethoven of the piano bagatelles does not. Yes, it is all music and ought to be listened to with care, but one hears differently in a concert hall than in a car or through iPod headphones. The intelligent listener makes concessions for all of these factors, ultimately cultivating his or her own methods.

A Listening Calculus

When attempting to think critically about a piece of music (on whatever level), there are three questions to ask:

1. What do you, the listener, feel the composition itself is attempting to do?
2. Does it accomplish it?
3. Was the venture worthwhile?

These questions intentionally become progressively less objective (the last being where "opinion" ought to be slotted), and this line of inquiry is (or certainly should be) the fulcrum of criticism, regardless of the level of expertise. After all, to expect the same from an episode of *The Simpsons* as you might from a novel by Henry James is completely absurd, because those ventures—as good or bad as you might find them—have completely different aims. It is ludicrous even to draw a comparison. The same goes for expecting out of Tchaikovsky what you might expect out of Richard Wagner (or the Beatles or Charles Mingus or The Who).

Even though analysis is a creative venture, with no one "right" way to do it, there are accepted techniques and an involved vocabulary which make for a more thorough, more adept listener—you can go as deep as you like into this, but it is not necessary for understanding. When reading poetry, for example, one can seek the deepest traditional root, understand the instincts of the poet, delve into the technical mechanisms, or one can simply—with a quick introduction—allow oneself the enjoyment one gets from a slightly careful, enthusiastic reading. The same holds true for music. Musicians analyze in order to discover the technique behind the piece, its architecture, its intent, its design; lay listeners need only to sort out why the piece works, what makes it cool (or moving or beautiful or sensual or whatever).

With each of the seven chapters of this book, we will examine these questions as they relate to specific pieces—or at least the first question, aiming to understand what the piece (though not necessarily the composer) sets out to accomplish, because it is the most objective of the three. The other two—did the work accomplish what it set out to do? was it worth it?—are the conclusions you the listener will answer for yourself; they will be your informed opinion. The aim is not to persuade you of the music's merits nor to help you smash the idols, but to help you in better answering the three questions outlined above. *Listening is a nonstop process: you can never do it too deeply or too well.*

How to Use This Book

This book gives you the tools in the form of blow-by-blow descriptions of the works. It is best to listen to the piece once without the walkthroughs, developing your own opinions about it (beyond "I like this" or its opposite). When you do this, *really listen;* do nothing else. Is the music coming into clearer view for you as you do this? Then, knowing the piece a little, skim the text—much of what is discussed lives in your memory now. Now go and listen, trying to follow the points using the text. Feel free to disagree; I am hardly always right. It is also important to remember that all the metaphors used are stabs in the dark, as valuable (or not) as any you might create. Do not feel hewn to them; I encourage you to freely deviate. Once you have engaged the piece on this level, give it another listen without the text. Do not worry about whether or not you *like* it, or even if you *get* it—the point now is that you have given it some appropriate attention, and are now possessed of an educated opinion.

Romeo and Juliet Overture

In 1869, the then well-known composer Mily Balakirev came to Moscow to persuade the twenty-nine-year-old Pyotr Ilyich Tchaikovsky to write an overture on Shakespeare's *Romeo and Juliet*. Balakirev had already been offered the commission, but did not wish to undertake it. He must have felt the need to tread lightly with the younger composer. Balakirev was a member of a composer's collective, known variously as The Mighty Five and The Mighty Handful, whose members included Rimsky-Korsakov (of *Scheherazade* fame) and Mussorgsky (composer of *Boris Godunov* and *Pictures at an Exhibition*). Though already famous, Tchaikovsky was also terribly insecure, and his exclusion from this club was distressing. Ironically, the reason Tchaikovsky was kept out of the group was his formal training. The members of the Mighty Five/Handful were deeply invested in folk music and therefore suspicious of Tchaikovsky's penchant for old forms and decorous melodies, and his affinity for the German classicists. To them, the music of Mother Russia—and *only* that—was the music a Russian composer should use. Regardless of politics, Tchaikovsky was offered the commission and, of course, accepted it.

Once under way, the idea of the piece began to enchant the neurotic Tchaikovsky. Writing to Balakirev, he explained:

> My overture is getting on quite quickly; the greater part has already been sketched out and a considerable part of what you advised me to do has been done. In the first place, the layout is *yours:* the introduction portraying the friar, the fight—Allegro, and love—the second subject; and secondly, the modulations

are yours: the introduction in E, the Allegro in Bb minor, the second subject in D-flat. I am certainly in no position to say what is respectable in it and what is not so good. I cannot be objective towards my children; I compose in the only way I know; it is always difficult for me to settle on any one specific musical idea out of those that come into my mind but if I do pick one of them out I soon get used to it, to its good and bad sides, and it becomes incredibly difficult for me to rework it or to recompose it. I am telling you all this so that you will understand why I do not intend to send you the overture in its outline form: I want to show it to you only when it is properly finished.

His insecurity in the face of the better-known Balakirev mounted:

You can tear it to pieces as much as you want; I will take note of all you say and will try to do better in my next work. But if you are hard on it now, when all the essential composing has been done but has still not emerged into the light of day, I will be discouraged and will achieve nothing. I cherish the hope that I might be able to please you, even if just a little, but goodness alone knows; I have already noticed that things which I have thought respectable you have not liked, and vice versa.

In March of 1870, conductor (and composer) Nikolay Rubinstein performed the work to little notice in the press. However, those who did write about it were impressed. One critic hailed Tchaikovsky as the sixth member of the Mighty Five (no doubt to mumbled consternation among the Mighty themselves), and Rubinstein persuaded a Berlin publishing concern to engrave and distribute the work—he knew this was an important piece by an important composer. Rimsky-Korsakov wrote, apropos of the main melody: "How very inspirational it is! What ineffable beauty, what burning passion! It is one of the finest themes in all of Russian music." Tchaikovsky simply said: "It is the best work I have ever done."

To musicalize Shakespeare in some fashion, particularly in an instrumental overture—and one not necessarily attached to any real production (much like a Chopin prelude that precedes nothing)—was not an eccentricity. Balakirev himself had done it with *King Lear,* and Berlioz had made an instrumental *Romeo and Juliet* thirty or so years before.

Later in Tchaikovsky's career, he would go on to compose works based on both *The Tempest* and *Hamlet,* excellent pieces both though neither has come down through the channels of history like *Romeo and Juliet.* At the time—the Victorian era to us Anglocentrics—Shakespeare was experiencing a revival, though his work (not the unimpeachable gold standard it is today) was often modified to suit the genteel tastes of the era (*King Lear,* for example, was recast with a happy ending). With such Bard-mania afoot, Tchaikovsky was *au courant.*

The story of Shakespeare's *Romeo and Juliet* may be familiar to most readers, but bears recapitulation. Romeo, of the Montague clan, is a listless, lovelorn drifter, who, at a ball, sets his sights on the lovely Juliet. She is a Capulet, the sworn enemy of Romeo's kin and clan. The strength and power of their love, knowing nothing of the rivalry of their families, is undeniable. Eventually they marry in secret, aided by a nurse on Juliet's side and a Friar on Romeo's, but things turn tragic as Romeo's best friend, Mercutio, slays Juliet's cousin Tybalt in a street fight. In turn, Romeo kills Tybalt. Banished and a fugitive, Romeo ingests a potion that will make him appear dead in order to put the authorities off his scent—but the letter containing this information does not reach Juliet. She finds him dead, or thinks she has, and commits suicide. He wakes, sees her dead, and uses her knife to end himself. The families, united by tragedy, reconcile, but too late.

It is hardly surprising that Tchaikovsky, who had recently married against his sexual proclivities, would cotton to this tale of forbidden love. We, through the poignant lens of history, know that love, in the end, was probably the composer's undoing. Whatever his emotional temperature at the time, he threw himself into *Romeo and Juliet.* "Here, for the first time," writes the self-designated psychobiographer (one who attempts to look at a historical figure from a psychological perspective) Alexander Poznansky, "he voiced the main emotional themes of all his subsequent oeuvre—the psychological drama of unfulfilled and frustrated love and of impossible youthful passion consumed by omnipresent death." It is typical Tchaikovsky: the music is part ecstasy, part eschatology.

An overture precedes the action of a larger work, setting the mood, swelling the scene, but without the narrative responsibility for blow-by-blow illumination of a story, which is usually the province of a tone poem. Typically, an overture is there not only to establish pacing, mood, and character, but in an opera (or a musical comedy) often it serves as a listener's introduction to the evening's themes—the tunes. In this case, as no opera follows, these "themes" become more abstract: they exist but are *sui generis,* relevant only within the four walls of the piece. Therefore Tchaikovsky does not feel compelled, even in the abstract, to Mickey-Mouse Shakespeare's story scene by scene. Instead he intends to set the stage by depicting the atmosphere of the fraught Veronese lovers, laying bare the emotional core of the work. To do this, he uses three distinct musics, cutting between (and through) them as he sees fit. These moods are (1) a theme to depict the moony Romeo's lovelorn "sighing," (2) a true, unabashed (and so famous you don't yet know how well you know it) "love" theme, and (3) a bellicose, hot-blooded "war" tattoo to illustrate the conflict betwixt the Capulets and Montagues.

The twenty-minute-long overture begins with a prelude, a mini-overture to an overture. The mood Shakespeare sets in the prologue is fraught:

> Two households, both alike in dignity,
> In fair Verona, where we lay our scene,
> From ancient grudge break to new mutiny,
> Where civil blood makes civil hands unclean.
> From forth the fatal loins of these two foes
> A pair of star-cross'd lovers take their life;
> Whole misadventured piteous overthrows
> Do with their death bury their parents' strife.
> The fearful passage of their death-mark'd love,
> And the continuance of their parents' rage,
> Which, but their children's end, nought could remove,
> Is now the two hours' traffic of our stage;
> The which if you with patient ears attend,
> What here shall miss, our toil shall strive to mend.

The corresponding mood Tchaikovsky sets is edgy but tinged with sadness, almost out Shakespeare-ing Shakespeare. Low woodwinds play heaving, open-sounding chords reminiscent of Renaissance harmony (but by no means a quotation or a pastiche)—the "mood" theme. This is the world of Shakespeare's imagined Verona as envisaged through the eyes and ears of the Russo-Germanic Tchaikovsky. The sound is dry, distant, cold, a frost on the landscape. When the composer departs from this reedy texture, at 0:37, it only makes matters worse: low basses and cellos form the basis for a cumulative chord, one that builds up through the throatiest bits of the orchestra, ending with the horn. The sound is piquant, dark, and bleak. And though the work is marked in the key of A major—or perhaps the related C-sharp minor, we are not yet sure—the fact that it does not quite settle on a home key for some time contributes to its discontent. Scary times have settled over the land; war and its attendant effects are always cruel.

At 1:12, Tchaikovsky gives us reason to hope. The stark quality of the opening gives way to a more lavish, "prettier" sound favored by cascading thirds—the "sigh" motive—which culminates at 1:36 with a high, held chord in the winds while the harp, introduced for the first time, climbs high, the inhale to the prior wistful exhale. Love is not in the air for poor, darling young Romeo, and its absence weighs heavily on him—symbolized by the sweet Renaissance-tinged tones from the harp. And though the music keeps climbing to a wheezy, empty, unsatisfied chord (dominated by flat-hued flutes, which are instructed to play inexpressively), in each of four attempts Tchaikovsky thwarts it with Romeo's heaving sighs in the harp. Romeo, in the words of the poet, can't get no satisfaction.

At 2:08, very quiet *pizzicato* (plucked) strings herald the start of a new section, or seem to—but really, Tchaikovsky just activates the mood theme with a pulse. Where before it read as cold, distant, foreign, it is now imbued with a greater sense of purpose, of direction, which Tchaikovsky uses to make the moment at 2:46—a direct repeat of the heaving buildup of 0:37—even starker by contrast, as if the will to live has once again been disturbed. As was the case before, this segues balefully into the "sigh" motive, which is in turn again followed by the same icy high chords and Romeo's melancholy harp (though this time, Tchaikovsky makes only three attempts at the ascent).

Listen closely. At 4:08, Tchaikovsky employs a totally new sound—a roll on the timpani (also called the kettledrum)—but does it subtly, under the radar. You might not have immediately noticed it, but it is key in creating the tension for the next section. Though this music is vaguely rooted in the mood motive, especially the reedy interjections by the winds, this is new material, something Tchaikovsky will use to propel us into a wild, fast section at 4:29, catapulting headlong into a tense, blazing allegro. At 4:39, however, with a smash and a roll he pulls back, marking the score *molto meno mosso* (a lot less motion). We hear the gathering force of the strings combined with the mood winds reaching a full, if pensive, climax in a key which is far away from the opening, a "lost in the wilderness" distance portending to great tragedy. Wistful love and death—the two emotional poles of this story—are cousins, and though they should not mix, the composer is telling us they will. Tchaikovsky is clever, though, using an "incomplete" cadence (the main note of the chord is not played in the lowest, most rooted parts of the orchestra). This dovetails immediately into the new section at 5:11—the first statement of the war motive. The battle commences, and "civil blood makes civil hands unclean" for the first time. Tchaikovsky generates tension not only by creating a music that defies cadence and key but by means of a rhythmic jumpiness, which lies in contrast to the purer, more "on-kilter" opening section. The real fire—and the real overture—has at last begun.

The war theme is essentially divided into two parts: (1) the caffeinated fire discussed above, and (2) a jocund (but no less manic) tune at 5:17. Could these themes represent the separate factions at war, the Montagues and the Capulets? Or are they two sides of the "fog of war"? At 5:24, the miasma becomes more gruesome, with some transitional material (built from the first half of war) chaotic and cold enough to have been penned by Stravinsky or Bartòk. War, Tchaikovsky tells us, cannot be clean. This spins into a cruel close canon (a musical device where the parts chase one another around) at 5:35, a *Sorcerer's Apprentice*-like dialogue between bass strings and winds, with violins fueling the fire. At 5:50, Tchaikovsky occasions the same bleak transitional music that introduced this canon, and once again uses it as a leaping point to take us somewhere new: at 6:03, strings fly above as huge orchestral wallops menace the texture, replete with crashing drum and cymbal. If to our ears it sounds terrifying, in the nineteenth century it would have come off as catastrophic.

Tchaikovsky reintroduces both parts of war at 6:16, presumably angling to continue the melee. Love—or at least the love motive—conquers all, canceling the chaos at 6:38. It begins—as love tends to—as a stirring, a slight differentiation. The transitional material from "war," once so masculine, so robust, winds down, wending its way to the bottom of the orchestra, and quite suddenly, at 7:19, the piece changes entirely. Romeo sees the lovely Juliet for the first time, and the key changes dramatically—in the juiciest way—from D major to D-flat major. This is a tangy, slippery modulation, the furthest possible key Tchaikovsky could have chosen; in this jarring descent you can actually hear the moment where Romeo falls in love, the passion that will lead to his undoing. Listen to the horns, which Tchaikovsky uses to create a glorious spread on which the violas (doubled by the clarinets) enact the theme. You know it well: the Hollywood "lovers meeting across a golden field" music. Stripping those associations, however, this tune intentionally resounds as the naïve *cri de coeur* of dangerous love. And, as every antecedent melody must have its consequent, at 7:38 there is the latter half of the love theme, not unlike a sped-up (or "augmented") version of the mood motive, chunky chords moving at the same pace (in music parlance, "homophonically").

This second tune, like the obsession of young love, leads with great erotic abandon to another slathering statement of the first tune at 8:20—with a caveat. This time desire has subsumed the second tune within the first, and love sings loudly and proudly, accompanied not only by throbbing, pulsating strings but also by a lilting countermelody played by a horn (not coincidentally the instrument that initiated the love theme in the first place).

At 8:38, love spins off on a tangent. It continues to rise, the swell of young loins, until, at 9:05, as if losing force, it ebbs. Instead of breaking away, Tchaikovsky tips us sweetly into love again. At 9:23, we hear one of Tchaikovsky's most sublime effects: the reintroduction of the harp.

What once stood for Romeo's wistful jejune fancy is now employed to play the consequent theme of love, a psychological cue that our hero's moony pathos is transformed to adoration. In the play, the lovers, declaring their ardor for the first time in the famous balcony scene, must due to circumstances part, but are loathe to say goodnight. In this recasting of their story, Tchaikovsky engages a similar effect using the persistence of the theme. As night falls on our lovers, perhaps bedding for the first time, the score becomes somnolent, lulling us into an easy, if soon to be shivered, comfort. We all know how this story turns out, and so this moment is both comic (like lovers parting, it resists ending) and uncomfortably shaded by the coming tragedy.

It does come, of course. If the piece—and the play—drew down the curtain on lovers sleeping in each other's arms, it would not stand as the emblematic work it is today. Alas, at 10:21, war intercedes again. The key, which had slipped from D major to D-flat major earlier, now slides down yet another half-step to C major. A cloud passes over our lovers, gathering strength and severity, and, at 10:30, the skirmish commences again. At 10:33, in what might be the unkindest cut of all, Tchaikovsky reassigns the horn, so recently used to slip into love, to play a portentous rallying cry, bleating the second half of war while strings scamper madly beneath. At 10:42, there are off-rhythm crunches, hinting at the first half of war. Forces are being marshaled; the love theme was a curt interruption to the cruel conflict. Pitilessly, at 10:55, Tchaikovsky employs mood entirely in the service of war, cast in the treacherous horns. All of Verona, including the hapless Romeo, must rise and fight. At 11:04, war returns, or at least part of it does. By 11:40, war is undeniable, and by 12:36, Tchaikovsky, choosing not to take a turn for the better, repeats war directly, in its original key, with all of its attendant sub-themes and transitions. Violence, not love, conquers all.

When we finally reach 12:56, after the confusing crush of battle, there is a hint of humanity amidst the chaos: with strings pushed down to a quick-but-quiet accompanying figure, Tchaikovsky re-introduces the second part of love in the oboes, as if, through the smoky turmoil, amorous thoughts invade the field of battle. It is a breath of fresh feeling, and gathers momentum and support from the rest of the orchestra until, at 13:39, in a great orgasmic rush, the famous love theme glisteningly re-emerges, evanescent and much missed—but now in D major, the key of "war." Love versus war; war versus love. Who, in the end, will win? At 14:24, it appears love will have the final say, as Tchaikovsky restates it grandly—but something feels out of whack, off base, wrong. Yes, the tune is there, in full orchestral glory; yes, this moment has been aided by a buildup of undulating brass and winds; but somehow, the explosion seems forced, inchoate, tinged with blacker possibilities.

The saddest moment in the work is at 14:41 when the love theme shatters. Beats of a foolish imperial consistency form the background, while in the foreground love has been hijacked and is slowly, woefully, edging on condemned. By 14:59, the triplets from before, once erotically charged, now teem with the powerful lust of the conqueror, while above it love is utterly subjugated. The horn sounds the rallying cry; love has moved completely into darkness. That is, until 15:13, when it is once again wrested from the clutches of war. Now we experience the true "love versus death" ethos of the work. We are still minutes from the end, which in the Tchaikovsky "turn on a dime" universe means that anything—anything—could happen.

As quickly as it reappeared, at 15:23 love is slammed violently into submission. It struggles for life, reasserting itself, but by 15:32, war has conquered fully, returning in its original key (though we have been on this tonal turf through most of this section, so the odds of a victory for love were slim). All hope has been dashed. At 15:38, mood returns, more militaristic than ever—we come to understand, through this bit of musical sleight-of-hand, that it was no different from war all along. Tchaikovsky heats the emotional temperature to the boiling point, excitedly adventuring higher and higher iterations of war, until landing, at 16:34, on one of the more frightening textures in the whole work: a terrifying smack on a low timpani doubled by seething basses and cellos, followed by a silence impregnated by the terrible realization that Romeo and Juliet will die. Love is now twisted its blackest hue as Tchaikovsky brutally employs a noodling, sinister version of it above a cruel march-like motive, a condemned two-step to the gallows. The lovers, and with them love itself, die.

As Tchaikovsky chose to open his piece with a prelude, he concludes, symmetrically, with a postlude: at 17:20, in the new-found key of B major, he invokes the wistful mood yet again, and sadly reminds the listener of Romeo at 18:10 simply by using, for one last set of heaving sighs, the harp, the signature instrument. At 18:18, he reminds us of Juliet with a final glance at love, which, though sodden with tragedy, is not without hope. At 18:52, he twists the knife one last time, sweeping away everything with a blunt suffusion of war. This backward glance at the opening, a swelling contingent on all we have learned from this great, complex piece, is very much modeled after Shakespeare, who closed his play thus:

> A glooming peace this morning with it brings;
> The sun, for sorrow, will not show his head:
> Go hence, to have more talk of these sad things;
> Some shall be pardon'd, and some punished:
> For never was a story of more woe
> Than this of Juliet and her Romeo.

Symphony No. 4

CD 2, Tracks I and 2 (Movements I and IV)

"It is a paradoxical fact," writes Tchaikovsky's psychobiographer Alexander Poznansky, "that Tchaikovsky's tragicomic marriage and his hysterical breakdown proved to be, in the final analysis, beneficial." Perhaps exiting his for-show wedlock inspired the neurasthenic composer. Regardless of the impact on musical posterity, times were certainly hard for him. "Only a month after falling ill," Poznansky continues, "on 24 September 1877, he informed Mrs. Von Meck that he had resumed work on his Fourth Symphony." The premiere was a success—at least according to the overprotective friends of the fragile composer, who was not in the house the following February when Nikolay Rubinstein led the orchestra at the Russian Musical Society, helming the world's introduction to this enduring work. The same Mrs. Von Meck, the composer's best friend, wrote, "There was much applause, and at the end the audience was calling for you and Rubinstein must have had to come out. I did not see because I was already on my way outside."

The truth of the situation was more complex. The symphony was only moderately well received, but the composer was so prone to collapse that someone close to him needed to soothe his jittery nerves. Reactions were mixed, though one critic hailed it "the pure creation of an artful master possessing the entire palate of luxuriant musical colors." The work was by anyone's account (even detractors) a step forward for the composer, who was entering his final phase and, as the cliché would have it, at the height of his powers.

Like the Sixth Symphony (discussed in chapter 7), this work contains a "secret program," a surreptitious story that guides it, one which the composer did not wish to reveal. Perhaps to do so would be to enter the then hotly debated realm of program (narrative) versus absolute (pure) music, a German argument from which this composer managed to shy. But there is something more than music to this symphony, something not reasoned out or guessed at but palpably sewn into the work: "the implacability of fate—the very idea that had become his personal obsession during the preceding year," according to Poznansky. During the composition of this symphony, Tchaikovsky wrote a letter to Mrs. Von Meck in which he admitted to finding the race of man to be ruled by a "fateful force, which impedes the impulse towards the happiness of reaching one's goal, which jealously ensures that prosperity and peace are never complete and cloudless, which hangs overhead like a sword of Damocles and steadily and continually poisons the soul. It is invincible, and you will need to overpower it." From the perspective of his own bleak implacability, Tchaikovsky, by way of this symphony, hazards some gloomy waters—but not without a concealed, faint glimmer of hope.

I. Andante sostenuto—Moderato con anima
CD 2, Track 1

Prepare yourself for some strange musical imaginings in this movement, a deceptive, iconoclastic, and breathtaking musical panel, one of the most sprawling and epic scenes Tchaikovsky ever made. If you have preconceptions about a "classical" symphony and how it ought to go, best leave them at the door, as in this movement Tchaikovsky hews to no rules other than the neurotic dominion of his vivid imagination. This is a force he certainly unleashes, composing a piece to which firebrands like Berlioz, Wagner, or Strauss would happily have affixed their names. This is not to say that the movement lacks form—quite the contrary. This is the opening movement of a symphony, complete with attendant statements, recapitulations, developments, and returns. To lament the degree to which Tchaikovsky does *not* feel obligated to the great symphonists before him defeats the potency of the material. Instead, this is a work in which one idea births another, or where the moving instant of the present preys on the immediate past, often in the most delightfully unexpected ways. Therefore a more prosaic nomenclature is needed to follow its twists, because this is more than a mere movement in a symphony: it is a phantasmagoric tour through an obsession, prefiguring Mahler's *fin de siècle* Vienna rather than a work of uptight Victorian-era Moscow.

For the opening act of his "secret program" (meaning unknown to the world), the Implacability of Destiny, Tchaikovsky commences with a herald, a warning, an obvious, clear statement that we are truly in the realm of the demonic, the realm where form does not follow function—where, in fact, it follows no master save the creative caprices of the composer's mind. In the particularly Hadean key of F minor we are offered a blaring, *fortissimo* fanfare—abandon hope, he seems to say, all ye who enter here. A lesser composer might have orchestrated this moment for brass alone, but Tchaikovsky reeds the texture with the ballast of bassoons. (Try though you might, you will not hear them, though you would notice their absence.) The color is forceful and sinewy—and downright unsettling. Another thing that makes this opening salvo so remarkable is its lack of direction. It hangs in the air, not rooted in any key or time signature. When, at 0:18, Tchaikovsky has this roaming fanfare—"fate"—land, it is on the note E, which functions as a "leading tone" to the home key. This means that, by the laws of musical physics, it cannot end there; something compels it on. We are not persuasively anywhere. At this point Tchaikovsky has the trumpets take up the fate motive, but as in the opening, their sound is thickened through clever orchestration, this time using the upper winds (flute, oboe, and clarinet) to enrich the sound. These maneuvers are all-but-imperceptible, done to lend behind-the-scenes weight to the blare.

The next major point of arrival, 0:37, defies key, landing on the distant chord of D minor (with added notes for bite). Every time we stop, we get further and further from any sense of earth, exactly what Tchaikovsky intended. He wants (and has) us on the edge of our seats, ears pricked, hanging on each note. The chord at 0:43 seems only to sink us deeper, but at 1:04 we are finally allowed a tonic, albeit one that feels antsy, unsure, cold. In the meantime, Tchaikovsky, evincing his sublime orchestral imagination, has the horns play unadorned at 1:05.

In contrast to their original casting, they now sound furtive and futile. Even though they play the same notes as the opening, they come off, when so exposed, as less commanding, less convincing.

Tchaikovsky then sets upon our stage a new character, a fleeting little tune played by clarinets and bassoons—the "fate moves" motive. This little gesture has within it some of the major ideas for the entire movement. For one, it outlines the interval of a minor third, which has throughout music history been known as the "fate" interval. Wagner assigned it this role in the *Ring* cycle; Beethoven used it to spell out the second half of his most famous tune, the opening tattoo of the Fifth Symphony—which is another work in which there is a secret program rooted in the inevitability of fate. The minor third, when moving downward, is widely thought to be the "dying fall" to which Shakespeare was referring in the "if music be the food of love" soliloquy. Tchaikovsky, in this small gesture, imbues his symphony with a musical archetype. There is also, at 1:06, a rhythmic device that is the germ of much of this movement's material. It is a rising tune, contained within three beats, which has an extra offbeat push to the fourth note ("da–dum . . . da–DA–dum"). It might behoove you to listen to this a few times, whistle it, sing it, tap it on the table, because if you understand this tiny trigger you understand, in the deepest possible way, the entire movement. And as this "fate moves" motive falters, loses its footing, dies out, a determined Tchaikovsky refuses to buckle, redoubles, and presses onward.

In what amounts to less than one and a quarter minutes of music— not even one-fourteenth of the way into this sprawling movement— Tchaikovsky has run the gamut. What could possibly come next? Time to dance! Not just any dance, however. A waltz—of the neurotic, the unsure, the terrified, a waltz with the dark, commencing at 1:29. Tchaikovsky picks up the pace, marking the score *moderato con anima* (moderately, with motion), changing the time signature from 3/4 to 9/8, which moves at the same speed. Where, however, in the former each beat was subdivided into two, now each beat is portioned into three. You will not notice this change so much as the overall shift in the music's character: we have moved from a decisive, brazen decrying of the existence of fate to an uncomfortable meandering noodle-like dance with the devil. Yes, we are firmly rooted in the key of F minor, but there is something so off-putting about the rhythmic displace-ment—from its outset both tempo and time signature come off as somehow *wrong*—that the whole farrago feels faintly uncomfortable, as if one wished nothing more than to decamp to kinder, more sure-footed musics.

Listen to the tune of this dance as it slips and slides, serpent-like, a slithering more redolent of Richard Strauss' German decadence than of the decorousness of the composer of *Swan Lake*. Though it is in many ways derived from the "fate moves" motive, the mild sickness of this dangerous little melody earns it a moniker of its own: "fate waltzes." Tchaikovsky uses the strings to build this tune, climbing ever heav-enward, sounding like it might escape the tightening grasp, but— at 1:51 when Tchaikovsky has the winds take over, pushing the strings to a subordinate role—this attempt at escape is disturbed. He then has these same winds wend their way, higher and higher, tension increasing, until, at 2:17, when we believe that we might be once again slapped down into our place, we are instead drawn to the fire of Tchaikovsky's full *fortissimo* orchestral statement. For the first time thus far in the work, we become painfully aware of the true power of the instrumen-tal forces at the composer's disposal. Nothing can ever be the same; these huge orchestral sounds rob us of our innocence. Moreover, the hammering away of the same two-note gesture that makes up the first part of "fate waltzes" is an allusion, homage to the other fate-inspired symphony—Beethoven's famous Fifth.

As quick as he forced this emotional peak, Tchaikovsky casts us downward, just as he did in the opening fate section. At 2:34, he finally allows a full, proper cadence (final ending figure). This security is fleet-ing, as right away he is up to his old "fate waltzes" tricks. He twists the motive into a puckish scamper in the low strings, after which flutes and oboes wrest the tune away, fomenting a dialogue between the top- and bottom-most sections of the orchestra, then mediated by the horns in a register reminiscent of the opening measures. Fate is attempting to creep its way into the dance, and everyone wants to get into the act. He vivisects the "fate waltzes" motive and passes it among the instru-ments until, at 3:17, he coalesces the orchestra into a stormy whole with two grand, full-bodied statements of the melody. At 3:37, just when the composer is gearing up for a third iteration, the wheels of the piece come off. The music verges on chaos as the strings, horns, and winds compete for the spotlight with blistering abandon. And, at 3:56, when again the orchestra plays as one, Tchaikovsky composes an agon between strings and winds. Using rhythmic notions plucked from the "fate moves" motive, they trade off antiphonally, aspects of fate converging on one another, ultimately collapsing back at 4:09 into chaos. It still sounds unflinchingly uniform, however, as if the composer is leading us by the hand into the eye of the hurricane. At 4:32 the music brings more hammer blows, although now each crack loses velocity. There are six blows—five and a half, really—that quickly dissipate by 4:38, shrinking from a formidable orchestral force to whispering clarinets and bassoons. This section is thinning; it appears that for now the rush of ill fortune can be calmed by a plucky little tune.

Nevertheless, just as it seems the music is snaking toward a desperate endgame, wheezing and failing, at 5:20 Tchaikovsky introduces a new motive, played by a possessed solo clarinet—"fate creeps." If the preceding "fate waltzes" motive was smarmy, untoward, eerie, this one is positively sleazy—a baleful character bent on luring innocents into a darkened alley. The forced jauntiness of the clarinet, followed by the flutes and a bassoon (a trio of suspicious characters) with the light "oom-pah" accompaniment, lends this section borderline jazzy ooze, though the material is drawn directly from the "fate moves" motive. At 6:08, "creep" meets a good chunk of the "moves," though on the terms of the former. Tchaikovsky is using both of these ideas to spin a web of musical seduction, lulling us with his sinister consistency. By 6:35, Tchaikovsky pitches yet another curveball by changing the key—to B major. This is a long way from F minor—a tritone, the "devil's interval"—and though the music here is lovely, Spanish-tinged, and downright decorous in character, the queasy modulation outlines its sickness. Gone, too, is the accompaniment; there is only unadorned "fate moves" goodness in a major key, a light teatime chat between strings and winds. Do you buy it? Has fate revealed its softer side? Is he now working for the forces of light, without guile? Hardly.

At 7:10, Tchaikovsky reminds us gently of prior storms, touching lightly on "fate waltzes" for a moment before returning, at 7:16, to a frothy woodwind avowal of the newly energized "fate moves" variation. Play ensues between this and the "waltz" idea, trading back and forth yet again between winds and strings. In the musical world of Tchaikovsky, however, delight and comfort are short-lived, and at 7:47 things catch fire once again. We are still clearly in the weird key of B major (less strange because it has been our temporary home for just long enough). The entire character of the work changes, though, building quickly to a dramatic explosion at 7:58—just the thing we were not aware we had been waiting for! Now, in full flower, is a new variant on our many fate motives: "fate sings." This is the glorious orchestral moment for which Tchaikovsky has been secretly preparing us, a full synthesis, a sheaf of all prior fate tunes, triumphant, heroic, bold . . . and, like everything grand or vigorous in the Tchaikovsky-verse, temporary. Quickly, at 8:11, Tchaikovsky pulls the rug, and instead of a restatement of this comfortable, strong motive, we face whizzing, ambiguous chaos. This leads, unexpectedly, to another statement of "fate sings" at 8:15. This was inevitable, but it comes off as a shocking surprise.

Now Tchaikovsky goes for broke, spinning this explosion into an array of endgame material: it seems he is fortifying for the climax. Can this be? We are still miles off from the home key, perfectly fine on the surface but subliminally distressing. This race to the finish is not only rhetorically inconceivable but comes off as tragic, a runner who believes himself to be winning brutally tripped seconds from the finish. It might be comic were it not so hopeless. This is another of Tchaikovsky's inappropriately grand anti-flourishes; our hopes are cut cruelly short by the brutal imposition of the original fate tattoo at 9:06. He does not go so far as to revert to the original key, which in a way makes it worse: there is still work to be done, he tells us, miles to go before we sleep. At 9:25, with a hasty thump, "fate waltzes" reappears, though reduced to a specter of its former Vienna-dark self. Whatever Tchaikovsky's secret program—and we will *never* know definitively—this is unquestionably a pivotal moment.

Tchaikovsky spends the next ninety seconds or so in the depths of uncertainty. The music has become displaced from itself, describing not merely a struggle to reach a climax but a struggle to breathe, a gasping for life. Individual lines crisscross one another; motivic scraps emerge, assert themselves, and fail. The bass line, more subliminal than palpable, descends punishingly downward. This describes the futility of life, the struggle to maintain composure in the face of despair, a feeble attempt to cling. A breathtaking orchestral buildup begins at 10:56 (another antiphonal call-response between strings and winds), and a sneaky modulation to C major—the dominant at last, the possibility of safe passage—leads us to hope once again. These hopes are extinguished again, at 11:33, by the relentless tapping of the fate tattoo. However, this is not the rude interruption it was before, but simply an assertion, all but subsumed by the "waltz"-derived texture, and it actually seems to be losing power. It is effectively silenced at 11:41, returning at 11:53 (but only after the strings, hammering away at high notes, force the issue). Fate is once again bested at 12:02, amounting at 12:13 to a David-and-Goliath-style victory sounded in the violins. This fire is unquenchable. It presses us onward to a triumphant moment, spelling out a variation on "fate sings" at 12:38 (with the addition of a spectacular countermelody in the horns). Eventually this hellfire is reduced to mere ember; "fate creeps," returns surreptitiously at 13:14, as if Tchaikovsky snuck it through the back door. "Fate creeps" is now in a different key, one closer to home, and while in the motive's first appearance the clarinet played the melody (now assigned to the bassoon), the material originally played by the cellos is now allotted to a French horn (who engages the flute). This is the same music, writ slightly darker—sounding more Russian. At 14:29 when again Tchaikovsky deploys the tepid exotica of the Mariachi-sounding thirds, they are in the current home key, a sanguine F major—a sign we are nearing the end of this exhausting journey.

Tchaikovsky creates a sunnier, more pleasantly disposed variant on "fate creeps." He uses it to build the beautiful musical spindles called *sequences* (a small melodic fragment repeated at different starting pitches), landing at 15:44 in F major. After winding up the orchestra for over a quarter of an hour, the composer finally lets it display its true force, galloping to the end—the final push, the coda—with inspiring enthusiasm, and not just for the power and volume of his forces but for a coming cunning maneuver. Caught in the joyous inexorable spin of a loud ending, at 16:26 Tchaikovsky imposes, in a moment of pure horror, the fate motive. We fall on our collective bloodied faces. This smack feels especially cruel because we could not imagine it would come to this. At 16:49 we are rescued from the storminess (in the Tchaikovsky-verse, cruelty, like beauty or grandeur, also abates quickly). "Fate sings" sweetly, with longing suffused with foreboding. Though this material is new, its character has been an integral part of the story all along, and below this baleful "aria," a quiet-but-mad scuttle threatens. Only in music can two opposing things be said simultaneously and be equally understood.

At 17:25 we have a new tempo—*molto più mosso* (much more motion). This accompanies a teeth-bared, feet-set, grim determination. For the first time in the whole movement, we *feel* that this is a work "in three" because each beat is heavily accented by hard pounding. At 17:37, fate rears—but it has been mastered, reduced to part of a larger texture. Tchaikovsky repeats the previous nine seconds exactly at 17:48, with not a single change, nailing the point home. When the fate motive manically reenters at 18:11, it is laid beneath wailing, frantic strings, and acts not so much as a resurgence but as a reminder, a grand coda, sweltering yet resolute. Tchaikovsky lays out "Fate sings" one last time, pulling no punches, landing in the home key and enlisting the entire orchestra to prove it, bringing us to a spectacular final thump.

II. Andante in modo di canzona

After the wild formal complexities of the phantasmagoric first movement—fate as a complex, multifarious force—Tchaikovsky will razor focus his sensibilities for the subsequent movement, putting a fine point on the concept of hope and its inevitable dashing. This movement—Andante in modo di canzona (walking tempo, song-like)—is as clear design-wise as the first was elusive, cast in a large, obvious ABA form (a *binary* form)—meaning there are three musical chunks at play: a melody, theme A; another melody, theme B; and a reprise of theme A. Lest the composer's intentions come off as simplistic, there are wheels within these wheels, tunes and sub-tunes, modulations and a whole host of other subtleties to make this movement as fascinating as the preceding, even if its overall conception is easier to mark. To audiences in Tchaikovsky's day, *form* worked in their imagination the way *genre* works in ours (*binary* registered to them as *noir* does to us). Of course, as is always the case in the Tchaikovsky-verse, when the surface seems overly decorous it belies the emotional content. If one sought to find a title for this movement, it might be The Bittersweet Lament of Cruel Fate or Fate Hurts or an equally purple descriptive. This movement is also a textbook example of how painfully sad music can be cast in a major key, defying the puerile notion that major equals happy, minor equals sad. Here, Tchaikovsky fleshes out the all-too-human idea of tender resignation in the face of forces larger than one-self—and what better way to express this than in a symphony, the most effective medium to communicate overwhelming ideas, long inscrutable thoughts, and broad despair.

The movement begins the key in D-flat major, an odd choice of place to begin according to the well-cemented rules of proper sym-phonic development. If the key is eccentric, the material is anything but: Tchaikovsky composes a beautiful tune—theme A—accompanied lightly by quiet, plucked strings. (The tune does not begin with a pitch but with a *rest*, called an "agogic accent.") In these opening moments we are offered the chance to hear, nakedly exposed, one of the great gifts of this composer: his ability to write gorgeous internal melodies. The tune in the oboe is beautiful, but if you listen—really *listen*—to the strings, you will hear a soulful, attractive song tucked away in the texture. The opening melody is repeated verbatim—or is it? What seems at first a direct repetition turns out to be more. The opening melody (the "antecedent phrase") is being "answered" by this subsequent ("consequent") phrase, and Tchaikovsky uses the set of expectations he has set up to wend his way smoothly onward.

The proceedings move quickly from stark to sumptuous, as warmly bowed cellos take over theme A; the oboe vanishes, wholly swal-lowed in the translucent rapture. The repetition is direct though the color has changed: Tchaikovsky fills in the orchestrational gaps, using the remaining complement of instruments to create a verdant carpet on which the melody can sing tenderly. Even in creating such a texture, however, he still subtly imbues it with elegant countermelodies: a duet between the cellos and the furtive, quiet flutes is a spectacular example. Eventually, perhaps having exhausted (at least for the moment) the emotional possibilities of theme A, Tchaikovsky carefully raises the emotional temperature. He builds a separate-but-equal melodic variant—theme A1—from his opening. It is as if the music has suddenly taken wing, a new idea forced upon us to disturb our reverie, a tune rife with keen ambition. Higher and higher it climbs until it ceilings. At that desperate crying moment, Tchaikovsky knocks things into motion, sending the strings whizzing around the throbbing chords emanating from the rest of the orchestra, raising our hope that we may yet exit the plaintive despair. And then things peter out. The strings find themselves defeated by a bassoon/viola iteration of theme A. They supplicate, careening quickly from perfervid life force to mild, textural motor. Within this A section of the overarching ABA form, there is a *sub-rosa* form, a direct repeat of the original theme. But one of the watchword tricks of the Tchaikovsky-verse is to lend life to repeated music by creating a scampering countersubject to function as a motor, which he does to great effect here, using the strings first then commuting to the flutes.

Then the unexpected (yet unsurprising) happens: another statement of theme A1, which reads as an interruption—until Tchaikovsky interrupts his interruption. Where before it seemed to cap out at the top, now, in a move that borders on comic, the composer deprives theme A1 of its desperation by deporting it to the risible high flutes, bent on mocking the tune's prior severity. There is a new character in town, and as it slides down from the topmost register of the orchestra, we can almost hear Tchaikovsky giggling to himself as he toys with our expectations. Where on earth could we be going?

Tchaikovsky slips seamlessly into theme B, without ceremony, and suddenly we are plunged into a bright key not unrelated to the home key. This tune is made of a dotted-eighth-note rhythm (rather than having two notes of equal length, one note acts as a propellant, a "pickup," to the next), setting it apart from the more foursquare straight eighths of theme A. For his new melody, Tchaikovsky employs the clarinets doubled by the bassoons, lending it a sound that is smooth and mellow but with a hint of bite, shifting to the strings, assigning to the woodwinds a countermelody reminiscent of both themes A (the agogic accent) and A1 (the upward push). The composer then changes, having the woodwinds assume thematic responsibility, heading up the third statement of theme B, while the strings outline a gorgeous, equally inspired complementary tune. Every good antecedent phrase needs its consequent: the strings play what might be called theme B1—which, like A1, reaches for the skies. Listen how Tchaikovsky uses the flutes beneath it, triplets adding tension to the texture. This is not immediately audible; you might not have heard it on your own, and yet strip away this background texture and it would feel vacant and hollow. This behind-the-scenes motion is responsible for the brittle potency of the passage.

Apparently Tchaikovsky found theme B to be quite powerful, because, after cycling through it twice (marshaling his musical forces all the while, fleet-footed woodwinds that suddenly make the texture into a juggernaut), he uses it as a kickoff to a grand climax, complete with smacked kettledrum and heralding brass. The triplets he used so effectively moments before in the elegant muddle of the background texture now serve as majestic glue to hold the orchestral moment together while simultaneously moving it forward.

Sadly, this is the Tchaikovsky-verse, which means that any good and sweeping moments must disappoint and come crashing down, and so the composer runs the moment into the ground. It comes to sound a wheezy, undone clockwork; soon thereafter, it has copped out, ceased. It is at this pivotal moment, just when we think things are at their worst, that the ever careening Tchaikovsky rallies, re-introducing theme A—without pomp, and of course with the usual subtle coloristic differences. Distracting from (or adding to) the foreground is a puckish tapestry of darting woodwind cascades. This cannot stop the inexorable motion of theme A, and so, scored for violins, it presses on, a verbatim repetition, winds aside, down to the pizzicato strings.

Where Tchaikovsky ventures theme A, is A1 ever far behind? Fast on the heels of this big return, theme A1 reappears, though in a castrated fashion. Where once it climbed to soaring string heights, now it meddles in the middle, unsure, fugitive. And a single clarinet wielding as its weapon the mighty theme A does it even more violence, cutting it off, whiting it out with a few flicks of the fingers. The strings, once forceful, supplicate; Tchaikovsky passes this new intrusion to the winds, through the oboes up to the flutes, attempting unsuccessfully to fly while the strings dissipate beneath it, dying off, floundering. Eventually the winds go the way of the subservient strings, holding chords while the violins outline the tune, which then passes downward, through the violas to the cellos, which appear to go off script. They sing an unfettered aria, one last gasp of humanity, a final outpouring of lonely grief quashed by a lone bassoon playing the plangent theme A. The winds try to follow, to help, echoing the strange harmonic places the composer took the cello, but to no avail. When the bassoon also tries to follow the cello and sing, the effort is futile. Moments later, the violins, in a final concerted effort, assay the tune—or wisps of it—once again. The bassoons sound the death rattle; the low strings tap quietly three times, nail into coffin. For the last moments of this movement, Tchaikovsky builds a chasm between the music and the listeners, placing fermata over the rest, a cue to the conductor to hold the silence as long as feels necessary.

III. Scherzo: Pizzicato ostinato

Brace yourself: it's magic time. This movement is one of Tchaikovsky's most inspired inventions. The title of the section explains three things: (1) this is a scherzo (a movement of a symphony, usually the third, in triple meter, a wild dance), (2) that pizzicato strings are vital to the work, and (3) that there will be plenty of repetition (an *ostinato* being a repeated bass pattern). But nothing within that title could have prepared us for this. For one thing, this scherzo is in two! To our ears, this is hardly off-putting. But to Tchaikovsky's audience, it was the equivalent of attending a movie billed as a romantic comedy only to discover it is really *Scream IX*.

Scored only for plucked strings, the opening section is a fleet, spry fantasia—though, like the previous movement, it has an easy-to-follow ABA design. For the first time in the whole of the symphony,

Tchaikovsky offers us an unrelentingly light texture, strings with not a care in the world—the composer is having a wonderful, smirking time. Gone is the orchestral hauteur of movements past; the future looks less bleak. There are two essential blocks to this section: the opening bars—theme A—whose structure cascades upward and downward; it is followed by two consequents—themes A1 and A2. The former, in a contrasting minor key, tends to stay put on one note; the latter has an almost Escherian deceptive texture: off-beats passed between instruments lend a fascinating, game-like confusion to the surface. Tchaikovsky spins out both A1 and A2 in various forms until he reintroduces theme A directly. A mad scramble, rooted in A2, follows. It is almost impossible to follow who is playing what; do not even try.

Not that long into the movement, Tchaikovsky pulls something strange out of the air—an oboe. He lulled us into the expectation that the entire movement might be string pizzicatos, only to remind us that there are whole other instrumental sections sitting the first few minutes out. He does it on the note A—the orchestra's tuning note, which uses an oboe. Imagine yourself a confused listener at the premiere: a scherzo *not* in three; minutes of quietly plucking strings; perhaps, just for a moment, you even imagine the orchestra is retuning in the middle of the piece.

This pitch bridges the gap between far-off keys, and here Tchaikovsky leaps with abandon to a distant tonal land. What with this modulation, the new instrumental textures, and the fact that the composer has marked the score *meno mosso* (less motion), we are now smack dab in theme B. As A was nimble and sprightly, B is courtly and charming; A (due to a complete absence of long tones) felt ungrounded and scurrilous; B is certain, almost regal. Immediately following this section, Tchaikovsky, master colorist that he is, uses an instrument he has previously held in reserve: the piccolo, which adds an air of otherworldliness to the moment. The dance then changes in character, becoming almost martial (played by the very patient brass and percussion). This is theme B1. Then the two themes—B and B1—are synthesized into one, a hilariously bumbling musical scene. The clarinet and piccolo are separate performers vying for the limelight.

Eventually Tchaikovsky brings back the pizzicato strings, who enter into "conversation" with both winds and horns, only to reassert themselves, returning quickly to theme A (and the key of F major). What we think is only going to be a quick interjection turns out to be a full repeat, and from this point until close to the end it is a free-for-all. Themes A, A1, and A2 are all here, chopped up, passed around, violently exchanged. When Tchaikovsky lifts his "strings only" policy, it is only to introduce chattering woodwinds into this theme A mix. Theme B returns—somewhat. It is almost as if the winds are *trying* to reassert themselves and their adored theme B, but the persistence—the ostinato—of the strings will not allow it. The two ideas come together for a gloriously happy ending, a coda full of decisive consequence and frothy satisfaction—especially for the nigglingly persistent pizzicato strings, who have the final word.

IV. Finale: Allegro con fuoco
CD 2, Track 2

Because symphonies are involved musical journeys, it is necessary to take stock of where we have been before we can understand where we are going. In the first movement, we walked through the fires of fate, crept alongside it, sang with it, danced with it, and returned battered but not hopeless. In the second movement, we mourned deeply, sang longingly, and came to a resolute—if sad—compromise. In the third movement, it is almost as if we turned our backs on all the horror before us, put on our brave faces, and soldiered on. This final movement—the Finale—is a shocker ending to a complicated, multi-faceted piece. It begins at a lightning clip, and hardly subsides throughout—with one horrifying, gruesome exception, a climax not to be divulged here. This last movement is the classical music equivalent of a "twist ending": brutally unexpected, but for which you have been consistently, unknowingly prepared.

It begins with a crash. Not a thunderclap so much as the startling entrance of a troupe of circus clowns, elephants and all. It is risible, because as quickly as Tchaikovsky smacks us with this morsel of gusto—theme A—at 0:06 it is awkwardly silenced, a rest that goes on just a little too long to be comfortable. Then what? A repeat, of course—this is really happening, the composer seems to say, smirking at his ability to shock—though not an exact replica of the first; antecedent and consequent. We must press on from here . . . but where? This is a place as occluded and cloudy as the opening was brightly lit and shamelessly vivid. A dark storm seems to pass over our heads in the form of threatening pizzicato strings, and at 0:13 the composer deploys bleak horns. The whizzing strings, once so vibrant, are quickly demoted to stormy figuration as we hear, in the winds, the eking out of theme B. This continues unabated until 0:42, when Tchaikovsky whips up a tiny bit of forced furor as the winds join the strings in their tempestuous flurry of scales. It is an empty, unsure, terrifying sound, eventually revealing itself not to be a portent of doom but a sliver of connective tissue that leads us, at 0:48, to a triumphant restatement of theme A.

Tchaikovsky gleefully stretches this new statement until 1:01, a moment where we might have expected yet another crashing theme A statement. Instead, he gives us similar material—we will call it A1—but he has compressed it into half the time, a diminution of his original material. He stretches his compression out, up, and almost through the roof until, at 1:22, what began as a capricious dance fanfare has transmogrified into a dire, key-eschewing wail, as stormy as anything in the entire work. At 1:31, it seems as if the composer, who pushed his material to fraught limits, is trying to wrestle it back to the joy of the opening—but his hand feels forced, pushed aside from a satisfying close to this section. Rather, at 1:39, we return to a variant on theme B, with a ruminative turn, soulfully Russian (including, for the first time, the introduction of a triangle, a small ping-y instrument not yet heard in this piece, infusing this moment with a fresh color). Beneath it Tchaikovsky reincorporates the stormy strings of theme A (as he did before), but now rather than serving as connective tissue they turn out to be part of the movement's hidden motor. At 2:08, Tchaikovsky turns Sorcerer's Apprentice, having the horns play the melody, and the strings serve not only to give the motion, but to push it up to frightening heights: menacing, sinister, robust, and gaining strength.

At 2:37, midst fire and brimstone, Tchaikovsky uses theme B to plead for sweetness in this Hadean morass. Flutes sing the tune, with buoying clarinets serving as bulwark beneath, while the strings, in the employ of the dark forces, seem to giggle with each passing statement. But as quickly as they were made adversaries, at 2:52 they are allies once again, as Tchaikovsky spins theme B into a grand assault that threatens to return to the dark place. This time, beauty wins out, and once again these gusto-ridden scales lead us grandly to a huge reclaiming of the opening joy—themes A and subsequently A1—at 3:25. Even when, at 4:19, theme B returns, triangle and all, it is now cast as a pacified version of itself, warm strings in place of the icier flutes, major key instead of minor. But all is not well: at 4:37, just when it seems we are about to settle into a third statement of theme B, above it Tchaikovsky threatens us with a wild, fiery flute riff, vaguely reminiscent of the prior motoric strings but more sinister. The strings portended tumult; this flute seems determined to lurk, disturbing the hauteur of theme B. It proves a bad influence. At 5:15, theme B morphs from a reflective, plangent song to an agitated enabler of the flute's diabolic schemes. By 5:32 the forces of light have been bested, and theme B returns to its darkest costume, played by the threatening horns in the dominion of the strings.

Nothing that has yet occurred in this movement—not the wild figuration of the opening, the uneasy fleetness of the strings, no storm, no demon, no descent into hell and return to earth—could have prepared us for the thrill, the terror, the shock of 5:53 when the opening fate motive returns. Our contemporary ears are used to cinematic post-Wagner scores, so an abrupt return to an early element in the piece this close to the end would not cause us to shudder. In Tchaikovsky's day, it must have been an apotheosis of sheer panic. In blazing, infernal horns (with winds doubling for extra punch) the wraith that has haunted every second of this piece is chillingly revealed. The worst has happened: fate has found its way into *all* aspects of our collective consciousness. Nothing can ever be the same again.

But wait . . .

When things were at their darkest, when a movement so steeped in frantic glee has wound down to zero, and the irascible inevitability of fate has sapped our will to live, over the hills, in the distance, could it be . . . ? In a masterstroke of deus ex machina, theme A1 gallops in on a white horse, fanfare-like horns blaring the tune of our redemption. Over a "dominant pedal"—a long held tone in the bass, the signal that the work is ending —the new hero rallies a *Spartacus* ending. All countries agree that a man's will can, in the final moments, win out over the tyranny of fate. At 8:02, theme A returns, a glorious sign of newfound freedoms, buoyant, imperial, and proud. From here on, every note is dedicated to the celebration, including the return of theme B at 8:31, which seems to have joined the bold revolution. And when the movement—and the entire symphony—slams to a close, it is not in the unsure home key of F minor. Instead, the work ends, victoriously, in a resplendent major key. The war has ended; the dancing can begin.

Concerto for Violin

Tchaikovsky's marriage fell apart, and to recover from the ensuing hysterical breakdown—as well as Muscovite society's whispers and judgments—he repaired to Switzerland. Divorce was simply not done, especially if the marriage had been contrived to mask the groom's infamous homosexuality. "He was tormented," writes biographer David Brown (in *The Crisis Years*, the aptly titled volume addressing this portion of the composer's life), "by the fear that he had lost esteem in the eyes of his family, and that they might no longer love him." The composer's fears were not, by any means, exaggerated: being queer has lost any number of men the affection of their peers. This collapse was the world's gain, not only because out of this emotional muck emerged personal understanding that would make him feel more comfortable with his erotic predisposition. "Only now," he wrote to Madame von Meck, "especially after the incident of my marriage, have I finally begun to understand that there is nothing more fruitless than wanting to be other than what I am by nature." In addition, this turmoil would inspire one of the most beloved pieces in the literature.

"I can imagine nowhere (outside of Russia) which is better suited than Clarens to calming the spirits." During this painful period, Tchaikovsky followed the course he usually took when personal tragedy struck: he set to work, no doubt emboldened by the gorgeous Swiss village to which he had decamped.

> I am very busy [he wrote] with the sonata and the concerto. It's the first time in my life that it has fallen to my lot to start a new piece without finishing the preceding one. So far I have always

strictly adhered to the rule of never starting on a new piece of
work until the old was finished. The way it worked out this time
was that I could not resist the desire to sketch out parts of the concerto, got carried away, and left the sonata on one side. However,
I am gradually returning to it.

The sonata of which he speaks is the Grand Sonata in G Major, argu-
ably the dullest of Tchaikovsky's works. The concerto, however, is a
timeless classic. Aside from a few trifles, Tchaikovsky had composed
relatively little since the break with his wife, but an enlarged tour of
Italy filled his well. (He even based a short piano work on a song he'd
heard a waif singing on the cobblestoned avenues of Florence.) After
his sojourn, he took a room, installed a piano, and immediately started
in. Within four days, he was composing the concerto, with no commission or performance. "Tchaikovsky's delight," writes Brown, "was
unbounded, and besides his excellent food, accommodation and service, he had a good piano available." Tchaikovsky felt a longing to write
something "slender" for the violin. It could be that a visit from one of
his former pupils, the violinist Josef Kotek, served up more inspiration
than did any of the composer's inner demons, because it was Kotek
who introduced him to Lalo's *Symphonie espagnole,* a single-movement
concert piece for violin and orchestra. Tchaikovsky loved it—he wrote
to his patron saint and best friend Mme. Von Meck that it "gave him
great pleasure," confessing admiration for Lalo's "freshness, lightness,
piquant rhythms, beautiful and admirably harmonized melodies"—and
wanted to do something like it himself.

So he began, on 5 March, to sketch the work. On 8 March, he wrote
to Mme. Von Meck that "the concerto is moving—not very quickly,
but it is moving." On 10 March—a scant five days after he began—he
reported, "The first movement of the violin concerto is finished.
Tomorrow I shall set about the second. Ever since the day when the
auspicious mood came upon me, it has not left me. In such a phase of
spiritual life composition completely loses the character of work: it is
pure enjoyment. While you're writing you don't notice how the time is
passing, and if no one came to interrupt the work, you would sit all day
without getting up." By 16 March, he had finished the piece—in less

than two weeks time—and by 5 April the work was scored, copied, ready to be performed.

The composer wished to dedicate the work to Kotek, who had not only introduced him to the Lalo but had done some preliminary readings of the work with Tchaikovsky at the piano (to the rousing approval of all present), no doubt a crucial help in the penning of the work. However, because of the recent *scandale* about the composer's personal inclinations, Tchaikovsky's publisher thought that the dedication might arouse suspicion, that the judgmental public might misconstrue his enthusiasm for Kotek. So Tchaikovsky dedicated the work instead to Leopold Auer, a violinist for whom the composer had already written the *Serenade Melancolique*. Auer was quite well known, and the composer (plus his publisher, no doubt) hoped he would introduce the concerto to the world without a whiff of scandal—they'd had enough of that.

Auer's full schedule—he had been appointed director of symphonic concerts at the Russian Musical Society—combined with a stubborn unwillingness to grant Kotek rights to a first performance caused Tchaikovsky's concerto to languish. It was scheduled, canceled, re-scheduled, canceled again, and when Kotek attempted finally to schedule a performance, someone with influence—probably Auer—blocked it. Because of these troubles, the concerto was already earning a reputation as unplayable. A young violinist by the name of Adolf Brodsky intervened, taking the problematic piece to Vienna, where, on 4 December 1881, he made his debut with the Vienna Philharmonic playing the concerto—at last.

> It has been my dream [the young violinist wrote to the composer, months before the premiere] to play this concerto in public ever since the minute I read through it for the first time.... How delightful it is!—one can play it endlessly and never weary! This is very important if one is to conquer its difficulties. When it seemed to me that I knew it well enough, I tried my luck in Vienna.

This performance in Vienna was the only Tchaikovsky premiere outside of Russia.

I. Allegro moderato
CD 2, Track 3

The piece opens with a quiet whisper in the strings, but a whisper that will come to define the whole movement—one of the most generous, expansive, and riveting in the concerto repertoire. From the very beginning of the work, Tchaikovsky's prodigious compositional technique is palpable: the kernels of the movement are evident within thirty seconds. Take the opening gesture, a quiet tune played by the string section—perhaps forecasting the soloist, like a premonition—which, when broken down, comes to summarize the whole capacious movement. It is not the melody that is the most important thing to listen for—though that, too, will come to bear—but the rhythm of that melody. It establishes the entire movement.

Each piece of music sets up expectations, based on the work's meter, of strong and weak beats. It is the placement of the beats within a larger pattern (called a *measure* or *bar*) that will define a large amount of how the music is perceived. If, for example, a work is said to be "in two," the pattern of beats within the measure could be explained as "STRONG-weak." "In three" would read as "STRONG-weak-weak," and something in four—or "common time," as in this movement—would be most likely to be laid out as "STRONG-weak-STRONG-weak." The opening gesture of the concerto is a study in strong-weak relations, and this sense of beat placement is one way to understand the whole movement. A "STRONG weak–weak STRONG" feeling, then, favors the tune; sing it back to yourself to get a sense of this. In other words, the germ of the piece—motive A—is about two or more notes placed on a weak beat leading to a solid landing squarely on a strong beat.

This exegesis makes it sound more complex than it is; listen and all will become clear. Reading this can feel academic; hearing and understanding it is purely visceral. At the "tail" of motive A (at 0:06) there is a slight tripping of the established beat pattern: the music lands as it did before, but forcefully on a weak beat. This notion—motive A1—will be spun out to almost grotesque lengths later on; for now, it remains buried within the opening sigh. Two seconds later, at 0:08, there is a four-note ending to the tune—A2—which, as the strong-weak patterns we've come to understand have been tripped up by A1, now feels both final ("cadential") and off-putting. We will see this again. What happens next, at 0:11, sounds like a repeat but is not because the notes are different. Tchaikovsky is letting us in on a little more of his game: if the first tune is a question ("antecedent"), this version is an answer ("consequent").

Suddenly, at 0:21, the basses and cellos begin to throb, to pulse, above which Tchaikovsky gives us another melody in the strings—motive B—not entirely unrelated to motive A in that it too pushes to a landing on a strong beat, but so different in character that it certainly deserves a separate designation. Now that we've heard it, Tchaikovsky seems to say (with his dogged basses as backup), the movement can really begin—immediately the music expands. Listen, though, to the oboes at 0:25, and you will hear motive A buried in the texture, transposed but unmistakable. Until 0:43, Tchaikovsky oscillates freely between motives A and B, all but eradicating our poor little opening sigh with full-bodied, incisive music. However, at 0:43 he wipes them out with upward leaping figures in the winds followed by an "answer" in the strings. It's as if the winds are showing off, so the strings definitively remind them that this piece is a concerto for the violin.

At 0:50 the violin enters unceremoniously, sneaking in the back door. It is a subdued entrance, but does not allow us to forget who the soloist is: after leaping to the center of the stage, the instrument climbs upward, ranging quickly from its lowest register to the heavens, touching on filaments of all the preceding motives. If both the orchestral introduction and the entrance of the soloist outline a rhetorical flourish—all arguments are stated—then when at 1:16 Tchaikovsky re-inducts the orchestra into the fold, the flourish is over. Time to get down to concerto business, beginning with motive B—with one important addition: a second part of B, an answer at 1:29 that again toys with the push to land on a strong beat. Even when elaborating, either with an ornament or, in this case, with a whole new chunk of musical material, Tchaikovsky never strays far from his opening notions. For a case in point, the next idea Tchaikovsky adds (at 1:41) hammers on the "weak-strong" idea with manic insistence, slapping on a virtuosic tail. At 1:58 he rebounds to motive B, but it now belongs to the violin.

In a sea of false starts, this is where the action of this concerto truly begins—and to prove this point, Tchaikovksy, for the first time in the entire piece, entertains the tonic key of D major, a "full cadence." The music is resolute: we, as listeners, are finally safe.

Just when you thought the run before 1:58 was simply a gesture, a precipitate of motive B, at 2:32 Tchaikovsky makes a whole sub-theme from this gesture, a lilting, jig-like tune, written "in three," which the composer utilizes to build to a quick climax at 2:59. This is lean composing, where even the most innocent musical device is fodder to be plumbed for future material, a concept which composer Arnold Schoenberg called the principle of "developing variation" (he used it to explain the music of Brahms, whose work Tchaikovsky abhorred yet understood). Careful listening pays off: any fleeting musical character can be turned around and made large, especially by a composer possessed of this level of technical prowess. For example, the manic "weak-strong" idea at 1:41, then played by the soloist alone, now forms a set of grand orchestral wallops that carry the music until 3:22. From precious little, Tchaikovsky creates whole worlds.

As the thunder eases, once again, into a brief (but blazing and bright) solo passage, Tchaikovsky introduces the second theme—motive C—of which Auer spoke so highly. It contains elements of all previous ideas: the propulsion to a strong beat of motive A crossed with the running motor drive of motive B. This new motive, to which the entire piece has been secretly building, is little more than a cleverly minted synthesis. In a typical sonata-allegro-form piece (a template Tchaikovsky follows to the letter) the second theme is in a key that is closely related to yet different from the first. Though this is true here, Tchaikovsky—always full of trickery—begins with a harmony that does not sit quite right. The music could never settle here; the physics of tonality bid it press on; this landing is simultaneously comforting and unsettling. When the theme repeats wholesale—after some gorgeous, touching work in the solo violin's topmost register—listen, at 4:31, for the cascading downward clarinet. It's a spectacular, Tchaikovsky-verse figurative touch, one he inverts at 4:59 into an upward flourish, exceeding the reach of the clarinet, passing the latter part to the flute. It is as if the solo violin wishes again to fly on its own, without continuing conversation with the orchestra, and so at 5:22 it does just that. The orchestra is forced back into its accompanimental role . . . but not for long. Part of the drama of the concerto form is the back and forth, the taking and relinquishing of control: at 5:38 Tchaikovsky bids the ensemble once again wrest command from the soloist, who answers with a frantic, motoric obbligato alongside another statement of motive C—one led not by the soloist but by the flutes. This eventually, at 5:51, turns slightly demonic, the fiddler sawing deep into the instrument with wild triplet figuration while the section violins—which began this piece—compel motive C in the middle register, reminiscent of the opening.

At this point, the music seems on the verge of explosion into chaos: we, in a short five minutes or so, have been tossed from opening whisper to lilting theme to orchestral fire and back again. What could possibly happen now? A thunderous explosion would suit the mood, something no doubt Tchaikovsky knew—and chose *not* to offer. Instead, at 5:57, there emerges a precious scampering texture, with the violin playing cute triplets above chattering woodwinds. We've moved from the fires of hell in the lowest register of the strings to a verdant, pastoral forest in the upper woodwinds, having turned on a dime. Tchaikovsky is thrifty with overt brio. Tension mounts; fires are refueled. Our spry little theme reveals itself, eventually, not just to be an inconsequential puckish dance—nothing in the Tchaikovsky-verse is without consequence—but is morphed into a device used to heat the emotional temperature to another boiling point. At 6:32, the high strings over low, almost Stravinsky-like chunk chords (built firmly and easily on the second part of motive A) portend once again an explosion. The tension becomes almost unbearable; something has to shatter. Just when one might believe that the culmination of forces will never come, Tchaikovsky delivers. At 6:50, emboldened by this massive upsurge, the composer re-introduces motive C, creating perhaps the most glorious musical moment he ever made. The fiddle stops—breaking down from sheer exhaustion—and the orchestra takes over grandly—ecstatic, orgasmic, and palpably complete. This is the moment for which we have been waiting, when all the elements come together; we have finally landed somewhere safe.

In the Tchaikovsky-verse pomp, payoffs, and grandiosity are always fleeting, glimpses into realms of beauty where we are not guests but merely tourists; at 7:26 he warps the music into a cruel minor key. Here he taunts the second melody of motive B into a slow dance with fate—a trick he learned from Mozart, his absolute hero—evincing his ability to sour even the most glorious of moments. His argument becomes moribund, his bent eschatological. Everything, he seems to say (in the most compelling fashion), withers and dies. The ecstatic theme was a turn-on, and once we know it can happen, all we will do is want it again—it has become a fix. What ensues both within us and on the surface of the music is the struggle for life. He pushes the string section against the rest of the orchestra: as they toil to breathe, he uses winds to pull them back to the depths.

At 8:11, the soloist furtively re-enters as if cautiously settling an argument. The tonal center is unclear; the violin re-affirms the material, playing, once again, a synthesis of motives A, B, and C, but the terrain is uncertain, the tone neurasthenic. But there is life left: at 8:18, Tchaikovsky re-introduces motive B, albeit in the now distant key of C major. It feels mollifying more than satisfying, a temporary, peripatetic solution. Even though it sounds bright and optimistic, wheels spin within the texture, preventing us from completely reliving the glory of less than a minute ago. By 9:00, the re-assertion turns manic, hammering away, an attempt to persuade the orchestra—and perhaps the listener—of the value of the recent orgasmic explosion, even if the fiddler needs to wander through several distant keys to do so.

Eventually, something surprising happens, especially in a work of Tchaikovsky: good triumphs rather decisively. At 9:33, there is another iteration of the regal, orchestral statement of motive B. But by 9:52 the composer has once again pushed things toward oblivion as the music marches steadily upward. At 10:17, we land in pure damnation, a Faustian conversation between an orchestra turned ugly and a soloist who argues for purity—a major triad. It's as if to say, "Please, it is my turn." Request granted.

What follows next is a cadenza, where, unaccompanied, the soloist takes front and center, not only proving his mettle technically, but also, in the case of this concerto, confirming the vitality of the basic

argument. Listen for music on a weak beat giving way forcefully to a
strong beat; listen for a calculated fast ascent to an impossibly high note,
reminiscent of the soloist's first entrance; listen, above all, for motives
A, B, and C, as each is there in some fashion or another. This is not just
a place for virtuoso fireworks (though there are plenty). This is a soliloquy, as in Shakespeare (another of the composer's heroes), a reckoning
of all the major themes. By 13:27, Tchaikovsky—after the usual signal
trills—settles on lilt, on motive B, and—at last—on the home key of
D major. With a mere seven minutes to go in the movement, we are
allowed some safety, some sweetness. The composer is re-seducing us,
luring us in with his pleasing tune. He is transmogrified—Orpheus,
perhaps. But the languor cannot last for long. The violin once again
takes off—but leads us into familiar territory. At 14:03, Tchaikovsky
repeats his principal theme—in the home key, different but not easy to
recognize as such—and for the next four minutes or so we are in a sea
of the known. At 15:44, we again hear the second theme, aka motive C,
though slightly changed. Before, it landed somewhere incomplete,
a final chord voiced in an unstable fashion; now, Tchaikovsky allows
for a more satisfying landing. (Listen to the new addition of a passing,
languorous bassoon melody at 16:13, or to the upward cascade of the
clarinet-cum-flute at 16:43. Even when he is repeating his material
directly, this composer never forgets to add details.) At 17:39, we hear
the fire from earlier give way immediately to a jaunty little tune at
17:42. At 18:18, Tchaikovsky hastens to remind us of the chunky low
chords above which difficult high trills scuttle. Once again, he builds
to an explosion. This time, however, we have him pegged: we know
what will come next. At 18:37, we *are certain* that there will be that
same glorious, grand statement for which we've hungered. That is how
it happened before, and since we have now spent the better part of four
minutes with direct repeats, it stands to reason this moment should be
no different . . . and in the hands of a lesser composer, it no doubt would
be, but Tchaikovsky uses some musical sleight of hand, the proverbial
"red herring." In a way, he's spent minutes lulling us into submission,
allowing us to believe that the second verse was, in fact, the same as
the first—but it is not. Instead, in this well-wrought moment of explosion, it is almost as if Tchaikovsky, aware the movement is coming

to a close, makes a mad dash to the finish line, offering one last new idea—though, as usual, one spun from the opening cloth. From here on to the end, we have entered what is called the *coda* (tail) of the work, two minutes of intractable, open-throttle motion, hammered chords, and violin figuration. No more need to argue—both the prosecution and defense rest. Triumphant, celebratory tonic (home key) chords resound, as Tchaikovsky allows us, finally, the pure satisfaction of an ending. It has been an astounding journey into many musics, a guided tour through both the fertile imagination and staggering technique of this composer.

That is to say: not bad for five days' work.

II. Canzonetta

What does one do after a rousing tour de force? Switch gears completely. If the opening was a celebration of major chords, grand gestures, an unfettered, fugitive design and rich melodic fragments, the second movement—Canzonetta (Little Song)—is about lean, almost medieval textures, a long, sing-song-y Slavic-hued melody, and a simple (but not dull) construction. The overall sweep of this movement might be plotted thus: intro–maudlin–optimistic–maudlin–outro. The intro begins with open, dry woodwind chords, regal, serene, penitent, prefiguring Richard Wagner's *Parsifal*—an opera that would not be composed for another four years. The Canzonetta opens with a quiet benediction. The tune is vulnerable, and empty when assigned to the winds; when it is taken up by the solo violin, it turns heartbreaking. If this is a little song, then the solo instrument sings sweetly. If, in the first movement he apes the German classicists, in this little song he allows himself to be completely, unabashedly Russian. The melody is almost a folk song, cantillation in the Slavic tradition of the Orthodox Church (imagine a bearded cantor singing it). This is the music of a cruel and cold winter landscape. Almost immediately, the melody expands, forecasting the second, more optimistic portion to come. (Listen when the flute and clarinet trade the melody back and forth, like echoes on a distant mountaintop.)

The second theme, played by the solo fiddle, is an antidote to the first: where the former goes up, the latter goes down; where the first is languorous, the second is more optimistic; where the first is in a dark, minor key, the second is in a brighter major. The piece perks up; there is life beneath the frozen landscape. It is almost Schubertian in its story-telling, but where Schubert would set a song text with a sad–happy–sad scope of narrative ("he left me . . . but I love him . . . but he left me") and use the contrasting music to paint his scene, Tchaikovsky allows us to use our imaginations. This second theme breathes, expands, soars, and tumbles, without adornment or schmaltz, backed by the orchestra, which here does not compete with the soloist but functions more like a choir in assent, voicing woes with compassionate consanguinity.

When theme A returns, it is not exact: a second voice, the doubled flute and clarinet, antiphonally counterpoints the solo "singer," like an echo. Here the combined instrument—a "flarinet"?—becomes the soloist's doppelganger, commentator, a secret voice, a shadow hero. Eventually the clarinet, in its lowest register (called the *chalumeau* register), folds into the texture, gurgling arpeggios as the violin continues its maudlin song above. Now the secret voice serves to push the music along, adding a slight variation, aiding the development.

Soon there is another iteration of the A theme an octave higher, which sounds lovely and arch—except that is not how the composer wrote it. In the early twentieth century, Jascha Heifetz, the violin virtuoso to end all violin virtuosos, established this slight retouching of the score—perhaps taking Auer's criticism into account—as an acceptable performance practice. Now it has become almost always the way the work is done, though the score still reads like the original. The choice is up to the performer now—and since every violinist plays this work, and they all want to be Heifetz, it is not difficult to imagine whose path they follow.

Eventually the opening hollow-sounding music returns, which the violin anticipates with a long trill—and yet it somehow manages to surprise because enough time has passed, and enough musical scenes have been painted, that what was happening only five minutes before has slipped from our minds. Yet here it is again, this regal, medieval set of harmonies, slipping chromatically around while the solo fiddle breathes not another breath, at least in this movement. Eventually, after a reiteration of this lovely, plangent music—which sputters almost to a dead stop, a dying fall—the outro crashes directly into . . .

III. Finale: Allegro vivacissimo

Tchaikovsky intentionally deprives us of room to catch our breath as he plunges dramatically, without pause, into the final movement. This gives us some indication of what is to come: something of a free-for-all, a movement that snaps and snarls, ready to pounce. A *finale* in a symphony is one whose lack of formal rigor is its form. Here, without strictures, a composer may simply have at it, getting to the ending—whatever that ending might be—by any means necessary. Since Tchaikovsky's most oft-cited shortcoming as a composer is his inability to work within the accepted forms, the finale is truly his domain, a place where he can prove his compositional mettle, turn his weaknesses to virtues.

Right away, Tchaikovsky throws a wrench into the proverbial works. He has the music land on an odd, out-of-place note, a B-flat, which serves to quickly—and palpably—foil the key, being yet another half-step above an A. In a short space, Tchaikovsky climbs from G to G-sharp to A to B-flat, and it is just this kind of tense half-step upward slippage—a motion called *chromatic*, which is a word related to the word *colorful*—that will define the rest of the movement. Also present is a faint whisper of our old friend from the beginning of the first movement, motion from a weak beat catapulting to a landing on a strong beat. The composer is reminding us of what came before, where we have been since, and what the idea has become. (It is not surprising that these small notions are referred to as the *seeds*, or *germs*, of the pieces: they grow up, they proliferate, they change, they fester, they die and are reborn, they bear fruit, they are violated, they succeed and fail.)

The tune is introduced—motive A—and after Tchaikovsky pushes it around through chromatic deviations, the solo fiddle, absent for some time now, re-enters, a Slavic opera diva, and for a full forty-five seconds the soloist insists on our undivided attention, as if the real star has at last signed off on the movement, deigning it to proceed. Then both soloist and orchestra begin a consanguineous mad dash, manic, implacable, fierce, and forceful. It is motive A with a tail attached, motoric figuration rapidly ascending—motive A1. These are the building blocks for this movement—though, as always, the unpredictable composer has a retinue of surprises up his sleeve.

Listen to those manic repeats. It is thrilling but also a little infuriating. Tchaikovsky pushes his material skyward, leaping between motives A and A1 with open-throttled abandon. But this is the Tchaikovsky-verse, where nothing is ever certain, where what would be a hectic height and potential explosion in the hands of a lesser composer is a breaking point where the music rolls back, tumbling down so that the whole thing can be repeated, at least in spirit. When Tchaikovsky bids the fiddle climb once again to the topmost reaches of its register, he again signals a change in the music—this time, though, he moves to a minor key, a common trick of the German classicists like Schubert and Schumann whom Tchaikovsky so admired.

From these repetitions we have learned that when the violin is pushed to its topmost point, it is a signal that things are going to change dramatically. So when that happens once again (immediately following a spirited duet between soloist and clarinet), we are hardly ill prepared—but who could have predicted what would come next? Instead of exploding into faster-paced mayhem, Tchaikovsky pulls back a little, engaging the most Russian-sounding fantasia of the whole work. In the score he writes *poco meno mosso*, which means "a little less moving," or, in a more meaningful translation, "pull back a little." And he means it. The work lands—really lands—in the key of A major. Not only does Tchaikovsky actually change the key signature for the first time in the movement, but the cellos lay heavy into an open fifth on the notes A and E, two defining notes of the key. The eagle has landed, and in celebration, the orchestra takes over, heavy as a Russian meal (or perhaps a German beer). This bottoming out of the texture—after the explosive chord, only cellos and the low, creaky bassoons are playing—allows plenty of space for the soloist, who plays low, schmaltzy, dark melody: another deeply Russian moment. This is a new section altogether, an exciting entry into the musical territory characterized by a new theme—motive B. It is not completely foreign in spirit, still favoring the familiar "weak-strong" propulsion from the first movement, but the whole setup resembles the introduction of a new character at a late stage in the game, a wheezy, murky-hued new character.

Just as one could easily get lulled into a trance in this new tempo, Tchaikovsky excites the motor, moving quickly upward (courtesy of motive A1) to the original tempo, almost as if the soloist fought against the machine and lost. The violin, perhaps defeated, accompanies the orchestra as the strings outline a determined rendering of motive B. The tune is passed to the horn, violin sawing away all the while. After some difficult exercises for the soloist—fast octaves are virtuoso territory—Tchaikovsky has the music do something even less predictable: it relaxes. Now he writes *molto meno mosso*, "a lot less moving." Once again, we are back in a strange musical land, motive B but with a few twists. Not only is it slower, more languorous (almost achingly so), and the soloist has dropped out—motive C—but a conversation ensues, with the solo oboe, clarinet, and bassoon speaking to one another in the familiar language of the movement's second theme, motive B. This could be a depiction of three aged Russian relatives arguing politics at the local tavern, and when the soloist rejoins, it is like an interjection of youth and promise into the wheezy mix. The violin trades melodic scraps with the cello, warmly echoing the optimistic reverie.

But this fugue state is not to last long: eventually, perhaps emboldened by the sweetness of the preceding section, the violin rockets once again into motive A—and in D major, the key our ears are seeking. Could it be that Tchaikovsky is gathering his forces for the final push? Not likely: it's a mere third way through the movement. But the rocket has already launched; the question now remains, where will it land? When the theme returns, it feels forced yet still beautiful, stolid motion to counter prior dreaminess, a controlled chaos, a smile too wide, a giggle at an inappropriate moment. And there are so many repeats. . . . Is Tchaikovsky, who we know wrote this in unconscionable haste, trying to get away with something, pulling a stunt to avoid the challenge of composing new material? Or is he trying to overcome his fear and sadness by ironically forcing an almost glib, almost twee, beautifully insipid little tune which keeps coming back, like it or not, a fly buzzing around your ear. Is this the height of laziness, or the splay of mania?

Eventually the orchestra reclaims the melody, forcing the issue, while the fiddle interjects some (extremely challenging) virtuoso flourishes. These fly by, one after another, until they seem to be stepping on each other—both soloist and orchestra grapple for the spotlight, racing for the finish line. It certainly *sounds* cadential, that feeling that the music is pushing to a close. But, of course, in the Tchaikovsky-verse, nothing is ever as it seems. Soon we land in a familiar place—motive B—but now cast in a whole new light, the key of G major. Rather than ending here, this key—which is related to the home key, functioning as its *fourth degree* (the "subdominant")—we must, as conventions have it, press on. However, apart from the quirky modulation, nothing is really new; this is motive B directly rehashed, including a quick acceleration when the flutes take over the melody as the soloist fiddles madly beneath. Soon Tchaikovsky grants the melody to the violin, which quickly relinquishes it to the horn. This feels like mad, drunken peasant dancing, with the floor being traded among the inebriated revelers. Or it could be the awkward, unstable dance of a toddler, represented by the soloist playing harmonics—a special technique wherein a string player, by barely touching the string at the right point, can produce an otherworldly, high-pitched, airy tone.

After passing once again through the plangent territory of motive C (another conversation), once again in the home key of D major—and with a slightly extended lamenting aria for the soloist—the soloist stands alone. Tchaikovsky avails himself of this unadorned moment to kick the music into high gear, so that eventually, following a bevy of repeated figures (which any self-respecting minimalist would have proudly composed), Tchaikovsky gives us the main theme in the home key. From here on out, the real finality, the coda, begins. The work closes in a grand rush, soloist trading hits with the orchestra, and eventually lands with a crash.

1812 Overture, Op. 49

"Like Elgar," wrote biographer Anthony Holden, "Tchaikovsky is best remembered for one of his least favorite compositions." At the same time he was writing his glorious Serenade for Strings (see chapter 5), which was music poured from his heart, he was also (as many artists have to do) shilling for money, writing a piece, according to Holden, to "mark the consecration of the Cathedral of Christ the Saviour." "That Tchaikovsky," continues Holden, "could simultaneously produce two such dissimilar works, poles apart in both spirit and quality, is a continuing index of the turmoil still simmering beneath the surface of his life." One work, the Serenade, is elegant, refined, brilliantly worked out, and far less often performed (P.T. Barnum once famously quipped that nobody ever went broke underestimating the taste of the American public). The *1812* Overture, clang-y, unformed, dashed off in less than a week, gets play every Independence Day, fancy wallpaper to boost a fireworks display. Whether the composer felt such extraordinary distaste for it, and its status as a pops concert perennial favorite has lowered (or raised) the work to midcult phenomenon, it remains not without its own intrinsically musical merits. It is, for better or worse, still a planet in the Tchaikovsky-verse. If you are bound to hear it every summer, why not become acquainted with its finer points—they do exist amidst the layers of hoopla—and enjoy the work as more than a prelude to explosions?

The *1812* Overture has absolutely nothing to do with the War of 1812, which took place between the Americans and the British (and is actually more properly called the War of 1812–1814). It is "about" a series of battles fought during Napoleon's invasion of Russia which mark for many the beginning of his empire's decline—three years hence he would be defeated at Waterloo. For the Russian people, his defeat and the subsequent liberation of Moscow was an important historical event. Tolstoy commemorated it in *War and Peace*, and it occasioned the construction of a cathedral—the Cathedral of Christ the Saviour—which still stands as the largest Russian Orthodox Cathedral in the world, whose consecration warranted its own heroic overture from Moscow's most internationally recognized musical son.

Tchaikovsky needed money and could not wait for the scheduled premiere in 1882 to get his royalties, so he offered the first performance to another conductor, a desperate and unethical move. The conductor respectfully declined. Perhaps he could not do the job in good faith, prodding Tchaikovsky to honor his contract; or perhaps it was due to the letter the composer sent along with the score that read: "I don't think the piece has any serious merits, and I shan't be the slightest bit surprised if you find it unsuitable for concert performance." Not exactly a winning sales pitch, even from the most famous composer in Russia. So the performance went on as scheduled, on 20 August 1882, in a tent outside the cathedral it was commissioned to christen, under the baton of one Ippolit Altani. The night, an "all-Tchaikovsky" concert, was a complete success, with the audience whooping and hollering—though some present did, in fact, share Tchaikovsky's own view of the work. "Among many laudatory criticisms," wrote the composer, apropos of a local reviewer, "Krouglikov said that the three movements of the Violin Concerto were so 'somnolent and wearisome that one felt no desire to analyze it in detail.' The *1812* Overture seemed to him 'much ado about nothing.' Finally, he felt himself obliged to state the 'lamentable fact' that Tchaikovsky was 'played out.'"

The work begins with a solemn chant, a mournful melancholic Russo-lament cast for strings, in the "heroic" key of E-flat major. This is a subtle touch, hinting from the beginning that though our song is rueful and unsure, victory is, a priori, secure. Tchaikovsky commutes the chant to the woodwinds at 1:26, using this departure to spin out a massive crescendo—not the last in this piece, you can be certain. At 2:06, things move from solemn to frightening as a whap on the drum sounds an instigator to war. But as quickly as this builds to a thudding acme at 2:12, Tchaikovsky pulls back, giving us a timid little marching tune for an oboe while beneath sinister strings smartly mark quick time. The tune is answered by tense, ascending basses and cellos, perhaps responding to the oboe's rallying cry. We march onward, regardless of cost. And this swagger gathers impetus, with clarinets and flutes joined together to sing the oboe's song: it seems Tchaikovsky is angling for yet another large-scale climax, marshaling forces for the coming scuffle.

At 2:38, Tchaikovsky marks the score *poco stringendo* (pressing forward a little), heating the emotional temperature. At 2:57 he goes even further, marking the score *poco più mosso* (a little more motion), urging a little harder. At 3:00, tempestuous Berlioz-style horns lead the charge, taking the oboe's sweet tune and fashioning from it a hortatory call to arms. This gathers power and persuasiveness until 3:37, when it culminates in an overwhelming crash, leaving the bassoons and low strings to ride the call out to the depths of the orchestra. By 3:54, it seems the exhausted warriors have repaired for a night's sleep, with vigils quietly kept, the prayers of the night before.

Ultimately, the basses and cellos land on a baleful A, a tritone—the "devil's interval"—away from the tonic of E-flat. We are truly in no-man's-land. But as it turns out, the A has a clearer function than we first suspected: to lead us onward, functioning as a leading tone to the harmony of B-flat major, the dominant, and into an entirely new song at 3:59—the familiar "victory" motive, which serves as a bit of optimistic bluster for the quavering Russian soldiers. It is a fervent pre-combat oration delivered by a determined general, adorned with military-style drum taps. For the second iteration of victory, Tchaikovsky composes a gorgeous countermelody in the strings, an optimistic call-response. At 4:30 things take a sad turn, battle being full of fear and sadness, a place where people die. By 4:50 what was once a grand march has petered out to a single tone—C-flat no less, a strange note, one not found within the key signature of the tonic, and one that does not fit in any harmony we've yet heard. Where are we now? At this uncertain point, at 4:53, the *1812* Overture, one of concert music's loudest crashing works, folds easily into silence.

At 4:55, redoubled marching commences. In a new section, marked *allegro giusto* (fast and strict), a new character graces the symphonic stage—"march"—striding along to the battlefield, guns at the ready. Though by nature this seems the perfect subject for a fugue, what happens instead is, at 5:17, after the theme is stated twice, Tchaikovsky exacerbates a single scrap of this new music, pushing it higher to the crash at 5:32, instigating a mad scramble—after which the composer, either heroically or comically (it is hard to tell), introduces the French national anthem—the *Marseillaise*. This probably elicited jeers from the Muscovite crowd at the work's premiere, who would not have been exactly keen on the French. In the heated Tchaikovsky-verse as in life, the Russians bravely face down Napoleon's army as the grit of the scurrying strings clashes epically with the enemy's catchy marching song. When, at 5:50, Tchaikovsky uses an off-colored "blue" note as an impetus to spur on a new, darker section, it is not only a coloristic masterstroke, but also a palpable bit of irony. At 6:14, march temporarily wipes out *Marseillaise*, but it returns, redoubled in strength, at 6:29. Tchaikovsky then puts it through a series of peregrinations that range from stately iteration to squeal to moan, so that by 6:50 the once glorious enemy's song has now decamped to a wheeze.

Inexplicably, at 6:56, Tchaikovsky introduces a wholly new tune, the "folksy" motive, complete with a ping-y triangle. This melody sounds a slightly genteel Russian peasant song, one seen, perhaps, through Schumann's eyes, and the pulsing accompaniment lends it buoyancy. What this is doing smack in the middle of the battle is anybody's guess, unless it is a signal that the enemy will soon suffer defeat at the hands of the mighty Russians—with a folk song to prove it? This is a bizarre bit of nationalism, and perhaps one of the missteps that caused Tchaikovsky to be so unjustly displeased with this creation. The music is lovely, but it seems difficult to fathom from a narrative perspective.

Nevertheless, the folksy theme continues to blossom, to build upon itself, to sweep as only a Tchaikovsky melody in the strings can sweep, and it all but wipes away the bellicose brutality to which we have just been privy, paving the way for the next—even stranger—section. By 8:33, what was once lilting and pure seems to have gotten stuck on itself, but this uncomfortable echolalia segues seamlessly into yet another tune—"folksy B"—which is as quick and fleet-footed as the first was sweet and elegiac. Where the previous used a triangle for a distinguishing whiff of native flavor, this one uses a tambourine. Like the prior folksy, it is not without interest, especially the scoring: Tchaikovsky has an English horn (a striking instrumental color heard for the first time in the piece) doubling the flute. This tune Tchaikovsky pillaged from an earlier failed opera, a theft made no doubt in the interest of time. (One week is simply not long enough to come up with this many winning melodies.) As this is the Tchaikovsky-verse, the spry little hijacked tune melts down, passing from flute to clarinet to bassoon to cello, landing at the bottom, which warrants, at 9:05, a small-scale explosion of march. Tchaikovsky changes the key again, availing himself of more solid musical ground so that even if the surface mood is uncertain, the subliminal implications are of pending victory.

At 9:15 we hear the *Marseillaise* again, an ambush—perhaps they crept up on the unsuspecting Russian army amidst its nationalist revelry. The battle, far from over, steams ahead, escalating at 9:40, pushing, stakes rising until, at 10:14, we arrive at a true blazing reiteration of march—albeit in the yet-again-distant key of G-flat major. Another tooting of the *Marseillaise* at 10:26 defies the possibility of a Russian victory: we are back where we started, far from the home key—but things are always darkest just before the dawn. At 10:40 Tchaikovsky easily dovetails into folksy again—but this time in the home key. This is the decisive moment. Were this a war movie (or a novel like *War and Peace*), this is the moment where the soldier, desperate and seemingly lost, thinks of his country or his mother or his sweetheart back home and suddenly finds himself imbued with the superhuman strength, the true grit, he needs to carry him on to victory. Of course, where one folk-like tune comes, the second is bound to follow: at 11:25, still in the home key, Tchaikovsky once again deploys his little Slavic dance, "folksy B."

At 11:40, the final reckoning begins. A low roll on the timpani (on the note of B-flat, the dominant), dueling scraps of the *Marseillaise* and march, and rising melodic tension all culminate in the grotesquerie we have been waiting for: the cannons. What happens at 12:16 is by no means for the faint of heart as actual firearms are employed, in a bit of thoroughgoing showboating on the part of the composer. Turn up your stereo: this should hurt. We know they are coming—many go to hear this piece just for this moment—but imagine the surprise in Tchaikovsky's day. Even stranger than the introduction of genuine artillery is what goes on simultaneously in the orchestra. It is as if the entire band has joined forces to become a single, all-powerful instrument whizzing up and down together, trying to stay out of the way of the gunfire. When at 12:27 the mania begins to abate (in a repetitious texture minimalists would proudly call their own), one might believe the victory was short-lived. Think again. At 13:08, a new celebration takes wing, aided by a full complement of church bells (perhaps symbolic of the cathedral this work was commissioned to christen) and a band. Yes, Tchaikovsky adds a whole other ensemble to the mix, as if cannons and bells were not enough, which invokes a broadened retelling of the opening hymn from within the unfettered miasma of the ecstatic orchestra. If the guns, pealing bells, and band are still not enough for you, Tchaikovsky has hidden one last burst of light under his euphoric bushel: the victory theme. At 14:14, in one last groan of nationalistic furor, the composer re-imagines the little tune, not heard since it was first glanced at in the opening, as a grand celebration of cause and country. If this obvious moment is still uncertain to you, listen to the horns at 14:25 as they loudly blare the Russian national anthem—if you can hear it amidst the clangor. After this, it is a matter of the loudest cadence in the history of classical music. Brace yourself; there is no mystery or subtlety here. The consecration is ended, go in . . . shock.

Serenade for Strings in C Major, Op. 48

CD 1, Track 3 (Movement 1)

"My muse," wrote Tchaikovsky in 1880, "has been so well-disposed towards me of late that I have written two works very quickly: (1) a grand Ceremonial Overture [*1812*] . . . (2) a Serenade for string orchestra, in four movements. I am scoring both of them little by little. The overture will be very loud and noisy, but I wrote it without warmth or love; it will probably not have any artistic merit. But the Serenade, by contrast I wrote from an inner compulsion; it is deeply felt and for that reason, I venture to think, is not without real merit." Later, in another letter to his trusted friend Von Meck, he goes on to say: "To my surprise I have written a serenade for string orchestra in four movements. Whether it is because it is my most recent child, or because it really isn't bad, I really do love this serenade."

The String Serenade began life in the composer's sketchbook as an idea for a string quartet, or maybe a symphony. In 1880, Tchaikovsky was experiencing a full-blown creative block. Not that he was not working—he was retooling the *Romeo and Juliet* Overture and felt burdened to do so—but he was personally tapped out, needed to write something that came not from a desire to make money but from an inner artistic compulsion. This Serenade came from his heart. "In spite of having decided to stop my composition mania for a year," he wrote, "I have started to write again. For as soon as I have no composition in view I begin to get bored. A pity, really! It would have been a good idea to refresh my creative powers." But the symphony he was sketching evaporated his depression, and eventually the String Serenade was born of these same sketches. He began on 21 September 1880; by 7 October, with three movements done, the composer had abandoned the idea that the piece was anything other than a large-scale work for string orchestra; he completed it on 4 November, less than a month and a half after he began.

Three weeks later, the score was in the hands of conductor and composer Nikolay Rubinstein, but the first public performance would not take place until the following October in St. Petersburg, where it was very successful. "It seems to me," remarked Rubinstein to someone present at rehearsals, "that this is Tchaikovsky's best thing." Later the conductor told the composer, "You can congratulate yourself on the publication of this opus." The audience loved it. It was repeated in Moscow the following January, 1882, in a stunning student performance that caused the beaming composer to write, "At the moment, I consider it the best of all that I have written so far. It was played very competently by the professors and students of the Conservatoire and gave me no small pleasure."

A string orchestra is just that, an orchestra comprising nothing but strings, a standard ensemble by the time Tchaikovsky came to it. A serenade is a musical work intended for outdoor use (or was, in the time of Mozart), usually light in tone, the soundscape of a beautifully clear summer night. When together in an ensemble, even a large ensemble (the more the better for Tchaikovsky), strings still come off as intimate—perhaps because of their association with the up-close-and-personal genre of chamber music. It is like a string quartet writ large, exploded from something delicate and quiet to something opulent and overblown, a thunderous sigh.

In 1880, the musical world was divided into two compositional camps, each of which surrounded particular composers: Wagner and the posturings of his "art work of the future" crowd, who believed that even instrumental music should outline programs or ideas; and Brahms, who stood as the rear guard, the keeper of Beethoven's flame, believer in music *qua* music, pure, in no need of lofty narratives or philosophical precepts to elucidate his work—the old forms were good enough. Perhaps life in Moscow removed one from these concerns, but Tchaikovsky, canny observer that he was, straddled the line between these two notions. In his programmatic fantasias—works like *Nutcracker, Swan Lake, Romeo and Juliet*—he was able to use music as strict narrative, the epoch-making program music of the Wagner set. In works like the Serenade for Strings, he opted to look back, with sheer Teutonic purity.

Not all were happy about his nostalgia, certainly not those with a nationalistic bent—Russians, some composers and critics believed, should compose only overtly Russian music. Musicologist Max Unger wrote that the serenade "shows evidence of the influence of German classicism and romanticism upon Tchaikovsky to a greater extent than the majority of his other compositions." This was not a compliment; he believed Tchaikovsky a retrogressive arch-conservative. "On hearing the first movement, with its heavily measured introduction, its first subject à la Schumann, and its old-fashioned second subject, a listener, unacquainted with the composer, would class him as a German Romantic reverting to archaic forms rather than a Russian master." Old-fashioned! In other words, without the proper education, one might make the ghastly mistake of confusing Tchaikovsky with the likes of Brahms, no doubt to the anguish of progressives and their discontents.

For his nod to the traditional classicism—German classicism— Tchaikovsky chose to work within the confines of that old chestnut, sonata form. This is a complex design, employed by any number of composers ranging from Haydn to Mozart to Beethoven to Brahms, each of whom abused its parameters in their own individualistic fashion. The form, essentially, is rooted in a seemingly simple notion. Three parts—exposition, development, and recapitulation—outline its basic sections. Within the exposition, two contrasting themes are presented. They are then played out during the development section—and it is in this second area that composers really prove their mettle: the theme is manipulated, inverted, forced into different keys, chopped to pieces, stitched together again, and eventually, in the closing recapitulation, brought heroically home to the original key of the work. Sonata form is, in essence, one long conflict, a musical war where the material does battle with itself.

I. Pezzo in Forma di Sonatina—Andante non troppo
CD 1, Track 3

Tchaikovsky announces his intentions straightaway by way of the title. This piece, marked *andante non troppo* (walking tempo, in moderation), will also be "in the form of a sonatina." According to the *Grove Dictionary of Music and Musicians*, a sonatina is "a short, easy or otherwise 'light' sonata, especially a piece whose first movement, in sonata form, has a very short development section (the term 'sonatina form' has occasionally been used for a movement with no development section)." Thus, we can gather from the outset that this piece—in the bright key of C major—will have two distinct, contrasting, and ultimately recurring themes with very little to-do between them. A nineteenth-century audience would know this as a matter of course, and so would not be listening for the storminess of the no-holds-barred middle section of the larger, more involved sonata form to which they would have been accustomed.

The Serenade begins, however, not with the first theme but with a rather mannered, stately introduction. From the full-lipped opening sonority, we know that this piece is intended not for quartet, not for a full orchestra, but definitely for the string orchestra: Tchaikovsky uses the meatiest registers of all the instruments—violins, violas, cellos, and basses—to create a triumphant, flourishing, major-key introduction. His material is simple yet unspeakably beautiful; his orchestration is magical. We are sucked headlong into his musical world. To make sure you do not miss it, Tchaikovsky runs down this material not once, not twice, but a full four times. However, taking his cues from Schubert or Schumann by way of Bach, each time Tchaikovsky states his theme he does something slightly different. At 0:26, he not only changes the harmony from an unfinished-sounding A minor to C major, the work's home key, but he changes the register of the topmost voice, bringing it down an octave. At 0:51, he pushes the whole ensemble heavenward, sweetly restating the tune an octave higher, with angelic results. When, at 1:09, he caps the opening section with a final iteration, the tune seems to have lost its will—think back, a mere minute ago, to the grandiosity of the opening bars—and, by 1:27, the mood has shifted from strength to acquiescence in the distant key of E major.

At 1:54, Tchaikovsky presents his first theme—the A theme—with neither pomp nor frippery, stating this "up-down, down-up" motive in C major. Though the key has not changed, the plot (and texture) have thickened—Tchaikovsky uses a registral setup similar to the very opening bars for this first statement. The tail motive follows this "head" motive, creating perfect melodic balance as the stalwart feeling of the first portion is counteracted by the livelier second. In the hands of a lesser composer, the restatement at 2:08 might have been direct and therefore obvious, but Tchaikovsky uses our familiarity with his recently revealed tune to skip the music into another key—A minor, where this whole thing began (an easy move, as A minor is directly related to the key of C major). Foreboding falls over the otherwise sunny music—a move Beethoven, undisputed master of the dark cloud, would have owned happily.

By 2:22 Tchaikovsky has modulated to the key of G major, the dominant, a textbook modulation for a second theme—except that, as we are to find out, we are not quite finished with the first theme. Instead, Tchaikovsky spins out the head motive of the A theme in a big, bold way: listen not only to the tune, which has modulated to the nervous-sounding key of C minor, but to the terse, astringent motion created by the prattling cellos beneath. G major is not our new home key, but serves as a portal to this weird, minor-hued world. Tchaikovsky is playing with our minds, turning our ears against themselves, against our expectations. Again, at 2:36 we sound about due for an exact repeat of 2:22, and again it is dangled before us—but ultimately we are refused, because at 2:45 the music heats up, flying high, and when we land at 2:49 we are handed a magnificent return to the A theme. It is Tchaikovsky's way to deceive us, to make us suspect—and even hope for—these returns, never granting them when we want them, but later, at the most unexpected moments. This chicanery is among the tricks that make his music so engaging.

The agitated figuration has not disappeared; Tchaikovsky has instead incorporated it into the texture, now used to propel one statement violently to the next. The intensity continues until, at 3:00, something shatters. Tchaikovsky has the fast, propulsive notes scamper from instrument to instrument—creating something of a "hyper-instrument," using the whole of the string orchestra as a single, frantic unit—held together only by the bass playing a pedal tone, a long held bass note. The melody is passed from instrument to instrument, but seems less pressing than the groundswell of rapid music in the background, and when, at 3:14, the pedal tone disappears, so does the tune. Taking its cue from Mendelssohn's overture to *A Midsummer Night's Dream,* this scuttling texture cartoonishly brings us to lower reaches and back again, moving from chaos to decorousness, the tempestuous character of the work giving way to a lighter touch—and presenting, sans much to-do, the second theme.

In many works composed in a major key, the second theme is cast in graver contrast to the first. If the first theme of this work is not without its lavish lightness, it stands to reason that the second should be cast in a minor key, weepy and bleak by contrast—but this is not the case. When, at 3:24, Tchaikovsky finally introduces his long-awaited second theme—theme B—it is even more buoyant and elfin than the first, frothy, ephemeral, zealously leaping between cadences. The key is G major (the closest key to C major, therefore an easy transition), the character is bold but elusive, and the motion is constant. At 3:37, after two iterations, Tchaikovsky softens its character slightly with the cunning use of pedal tones. This newfound softness, like everything truly joyful in the Tchaikovsky-verse, is to be short-lived: at 3:50, he pushes the music once again into a minor key—E minor this time, which bears the same relationship to G major as A minor does to C major. If the territory is unfamiliar, the modulation is something we have heard before, even if it was at the very back of our mind's ear.

Something strange and unexpected happens at 3:56: where another statement of the second theme might be most appropriate, Tchaikovsky brings back the first, but sneaks it in amongst the character of the second theme—though in the far-removed key of F-sharp minor. This can only mean one thing: we are now firmly, if fleetingly, in the development section. Tchaikovsky plays yet another trick on our memory. We've heard this music before, but it somehow feels a long way from home, not only because of the key but because we are hearing it in a somewhat new context. This has been well planned; the entire texture of theme B, with its motor rhythms and bouncy texture, was built for this moment. The second theme, in context of the great conflict of A versus B, the watchword of the sonata form, is subjugated to the first.

Or is it? At 4:14, the plot thickens as Tchaikovsky restates theme B, the whole works, an octave higher, adding an element of tension to this restatement. Will it last? He begins to play with the elements, pushing and pulling the material into violent off-rhythms, pitting scuttling violins against resounding plucked basses and cellos, seemingly asserting that though the B theme has, in fact, returned, it too will be forever changed. Eventually, at 4:40, it sounds as if Tchaikovsky is rounding things up: what had motion to just about anywhere now seems as if it is part of a clamor gathering to a sweeping ending. The basses repeat the note D, which is the root of the dominant of G major, a harmony that causes us to long for the closure of a cadence. It seems the movement is destined to wrap up in G major, not at all where it started. He sends the violins whizzing up three times, building a library of cadential clichés. The big finish is just around the corner . . . when suddenly, at 5:09, something awkward (yet beautiful) happens: there is a grand pause, a break in the action, and then, almost as if Tchaikovsky is forcing his own hand, theme A reappears exactly as we first heard it. It's a stunning moment, unexpected, plangent and sad—in the perfervid jubilation of our rousing close, we somehow forgot the poor, lost, sad soul of theme A, now mournfully reasserting itself.

The repeat is exact, down to the skittering minor-key music at 5:40, the grand reiteration at 6:06 with its propulsive figuration, the scamper over the pedal tone at 6:17, and the removal of same at 6:30. This is all familiar music, recast in a new, sad light—the themes have, over the course of the piece, come to mean more, like treasured friends. At 6:42, the second theme returns, but it has lost something, been subsumed by the first theme for one reason: it is now in the home key. You can view this as subjugation, with one key and theme taking over another; you can view this as synthesis, where the two themes join forces and skip merrily to the finish line. Either way, in the grand scheme of the work, something extraordinary has passed. At 7:13, once again, theme A reasserts itself, but now it is hardly a surprise. Eventually, at 7:57, the movement enters the final stretch, landing on a dominant pedal; certain closure is imminent. Repeated Gs (the dominant of C) in the cello push things on to the end—and at 8:10 we appear to be landing directly in the *coda* (tail) of the work, the end, the big explosive finish. Tchaikovsky, however, has one last trick left, a final twist of the knife: at 8:28, after a substantial pause—in which one might presume the work is actually over—*the music of the introduction* returns, vanished and long-since-forgotten glory once again taking center stage.

II. "Waltzer"

After the complexities of the first movement, Tchaikovsky allows us a moment's repose in the form of a charming, tuneful waltz. Here he pulls no melodic punches, creating us a section that is without an involved narrative, composed merely in the interest of sheer listenability. The movement begins with a rest, followed by two notes—two important notes: the note below the tonic (called a leading tone because it exerts almost a gravitational pull toward the tonic) and the tonic itself. But through his normal trickery, Tchaikovsky fools us, landing on the strong beat (in triple meter; this is always the first of the three) on the note D, part of a G major triad. This piece is unexpectedly not in C major as it would presumably be; it is in the dominant key, G major. A nineteenth-century audience would have noticed this. The tune, into which Tchaikovsky immediately plunges, is one of his best—and best-known—offerings; you have heard it before. What makes this melody extra juicy is the bass line: beneath a sweet, unrepentantly melodic jaunt is a sexy, slithery chromatic bass line, especially when the temperature begins to heat. You do not know it yet, but Tchaikovsky has given you, in this little imperceptible bass riff, a cue of things to come. This moment is a tease.

There are three pertinent ideas that act as the underlying "motor" for this movement: theme A, which begins right at the opening; theme A1, a transitional figure, mariachi-like thirds; theme B commencing right afterward, which catches fire from the faux-Spanish feel of theme A1, suffusing quick scuttling notes beneath long held tones.

In just under four minutes Tchaikovsky will dazzle us with his trickery, slipping recklessly among these themes, as well as charm us with his glistening melodies.

Theme B is stated twice, connected by propulsive scales. Tchaikovsky employs one of these ascending figures to lead us back into theme A, though (as usual) something is different: instead of the first violins taking the lead, trilling happily above, a second fiddle, doubled by the cellos, lays out the melody. The quick figures which served as motor for theme B now act as connective tissue, between statements, between themes, allowing us to glide smoothly once again into theme A. While the topmost fiddle carries on, spinning what amounts to a countermelody, Tchaikovsky repeats theme A beneath. It is almost as if the fiddle has been given free rein to adorn theme A as it likes: it taunts it, teases it, waltzes above or plummets toward it. It is unfettered, free.

What we suspect is a rondo (ABACABA form) turns out, in fact, to be exactly that: Tchaikovsky then unveils a wholly new theme—theme C. This tune is the most Slavic of the lot: minor chords chunk along beneath a graceful, danceable spindle which lies somewhere between the aristocratic parlor and an isolated Russian village. It is a conversation between the topmost violins, which descend, and the cellos and basses, guffawing at each descent. You might imagine a family drinking vodka together by a roaring fire, complete with flight-of-fancy-prone child (the first violins) and a graceful teenage girl (the cello in its highest register), with her wheezy, glowering father (the bass) nodding off in the dimming icy light.

Immediately following another iteration of C—this is new material, so Tchaikovsky wants to make damn sure it registers—there's a return of the opening material, with a caveat. Before when the A theme was put through its first restatement, the first violins soared above it, commenting. That role is now assumed by the viola. And, as the viola is a lower instrument, the pulses it offers do not so much soar as chug along—gracefully—pushing the music somewhere new, offering a fresh delectation. The viola struggles to become a violin, stretching to the top of its register. It sounds furtive, even laughable, but certainly sincere. Immediately following this, there is an exact repeat of A1, our little mariachi transitional material, and, as we have come to expect, it leads directly to another exact assertion of theme B. When theme A returns yet again, we are again treated to the soaring fiddle high above. It appears Tchaikovsky is coming in for a landing, reminding us of where we have been together, one last glimpse at his index of melodic wares.

But where before we might expect theme C, Tchaikovsky offers us something even newer: a pedal point, one note at the bottom—in this case, the oom-pah-pah figure in the basses—while atop he begins to round things up. We have officially reached the coda; all that remains is the close. We hear familiar gestures (the chromatic descent, glimpses of all the themes), and just as we are sure we are through, Tchaikovsky offers us one last little treat in the form of a genteel, decorous, backward-looking waltz tune in the second violins. While it sounds final here, in the context of the entire Serenade, there is still a fair amount of unfinished business: home key of the piece is C major, and we close in G.

III. "Élégie"

To a listener unfamiliar with the Tchaikovsky-verse who heard the first two movements of the Serenade, by now a few things could be surmised. For one, this composer often repeats his material recast in new contexts for a fresh sound. The other: when you expect something to happen a certain way it seldom does. It is with this in mind that we begin to explore the third movement of the Serenade, the "Élégie." To what or whom the work pays homage we do not know, nor do we need to. A sweet, calm tribute is paid in notes, and from those notes alone (*sans* backstory) we might cobble some thoughts together about the character of the honoree—if there is a specific honoree. In this case, the *who* is not as important as the *how*.

The opening statement feels like a spectral version of the introductory material in the first movement: moving in contrary motion (if one line goes higher, then the other goes lower), essentially homophonic (the same rhythm, with an expansive, stately take on the wide possibilities of the string orchestra). Only now, instead of feeling grand, as was the mood when this work began, it seems pensive, plangent, a little lost. The question, now that we are better acquainted with Tchaikovsky's techniques: is this an introduction or a full-fledged theme? This query is one of the secret notions that make the movement flow. What do you suppose—intro or theme?

There is an uneasy quality to this chant-like scrap; it feels either too long or too short. Though like the previous movement, the waltz, the piece is written in 3/4 time, there is something different here. In a conventional triple-metered waltz, the force of the beat ("strong-weak-weak") defines the bar. Should the composer opt to work against this expectation, the departure would be palpable. But in this movement, the meter is hard to determine. Listen a few times to the opening passage; see if you can detect where the strong and weak beats lie. It will be difficult, if not impossible, to do; Tchaikovsky is consistently playing with our perceptions. Each time the melody of this opening repeats, though we are familiar with it from the first iteration, it still slips from our musical memory—this is Tchaikovsky's musical chicanery, using a waltz to lull you into thinking there should be a consistent beat and then, at the opening of the next movement, thwarting you. It keeps the music vibrant. Not until the very tail of this opening section does Tchaikovsky write a phrase that is clearly in the proper time signature, as if laying out his hand. This is also the first time he has landed squarely on the tonic chord of D major—the other phrase endings were not only diminished in potency by their rhythmic placement, but also by their unsure points of landing. None of them were on the home harmony and therefore none sounded truly final.

A minute and a half in, we enter a brave new musical world, populated by plucked strings (called *pizzicato*) and a clear triple meter. The score says *poco più animato* (a little more animated). Now we really hear the strong and weak beats, though Tchaikovsky foils an absolutely clear 3/4 by having the violas, playing pizzicato, outline triplets, which means that within each of the three beats that make up a triple-meter bar, where we expect to hear two sub-beats we hear three instead. This is slightly confusing, and will get even more so when the violins begin to play the melody—theme B, presuming (but not yet knowing) that the opening material was, in fact, a full-fledged theme—since they play in a true 3/4. This idea, where two separate, strong rhythmic ideas bounce off one another, is called *syncopation*. It can be a fascinating groove in jazz, a piquant backbeat-like effect in Mozart or Haydn, and in Tchaikovsky it can throw us off just enough to prick our unsuspecting ears. This whole movement is about the play of ideas, a rapturous roller coaster of not knowing. It is strange; it is unnerving; in the hands of Tchaikovsky, it is manically electrifying.

From here on out, the name of Tchaikovsky's game is to unsettle the listener. This is to be no calm, reflective elegy; this elegy has resounding quirks and a farrago of strange musical encounters concocted to bend the ear (but not to beat it into submission). The melody of theme B, still in a proper 3/4, is accompanied by a syncopated pattern in 6/8 (different from 3/4 in that the measure is divided into two, not three, large beats). Add triplets to the mix, and this section comes off as subtly uneasy.

Soon a solo aria gives way to a duet as the cellos and violas, doubled on the same notes (to add piquancy), sing the melody just heard in the violins. It is a compelling conversation that pushes the music upward until the point where Tchaikovsky removes the melody from the violins—they trill above—and assigns it to the cellos. (Listen for the chromatic descent in the bass that adds flavor, as well as being, to the ears of the nineteenth century, a symbol for death.) Eventually things settle somewhat. Theme B is repeated, though now in A major (which is to D major as D major was to G major; Tchaikovsky carries on his subliminal ascent) and cast, once again, as an operatic duet initiated by the cellos, with answering violin. When the composer rhythmically locks the instruments in with one another—homophony—the material slightly touches on the opening: not a restatement but rather an allusion to a synthesis. Then Tchaikovsky repeats the preceding section almost directly, but, as is his wont, uses it as a springboard to new heights—the new(ish) transitional material—and, after allowing a brief solo for the violas, he wends his way back, dovetailing into a recapitulation of theme B.

Now that we are well into the Serenade, we are familiar with the rhetorical tricks of the Tchaikovsky-verse, one of the most common being the recasting of repeats by simply adding a little more information, a layer, most often one with a pulse. This third movement is no exception. As if the triplets combined with the question of 3/4 or 6/8 were not strange enough, now we must contend with scampering violins spelling out sixteenth-notes. It is almost as if the work is in three time signatures at once. Tchaikovsky also likes to bring his thematic elements together, usually to heartrending emotional effect, and he does exactly that. Violins playing in octaves, cellos carving out a gorgeous countermelody, the triplets adding a languorous pulse, all combine for a hefty emotional moment. Of course, these overt outpourings never last long: he thins the ranks, dissipates the harmony, so that only the cellos are left to remind us of the vanished ecstasy of the previous moment.

Now comes one of the most deceptive (thrillingly so) moments in the whole work. The violins, now muted, take off, and what feels imminent is either another return of theme B or some other climax we have recently experienced. Tchaikovsky gives us neither. Instead, the composer has the scamper of the fiddles peter out mid-course, leaving us in a captious, appropriately uncomfortable silence. What next? Theme B? Will there be a wholly new theme, revealing this movement to be another rondo? No. What we do get is a direct, exact iteration of the opening measures, revealing it to be a theme after all—theme A, named retroactively. The repetition is exact, but in contrast to the preceding storm it seems unduly calm and quiet—that is, until Tchaikovsky spins us in a new direction once again. Like a failing, erratic heart, the music heats up, goes irregular, threatens to stop again, a Mahlerian struggle for life (decades before Mahler). Then, in a sudden spate of counterpoint, Tchaikovsky has the rest of the orchestra follow the first violins downward, pushing chromatically to the bottom, bleeding all possible life from the instruments, until we are again in the familiar territory of theme B, with a pedal tone and its implications of finality driving the music to an ending. As a sort of "wrap party," Tchaikovsky tours through the movement's principal ideas: the triplets, the scampering motor notes, the confusion of what sounds like multiple meters. Like a music box winding down, things fall slowly apart and get incrementally quieter until we come to rest on the most mordant major chord ever penned. Then, phoenix-like, Tchaikovsky rouses us from our collective despair with a glimmer of hope: when we believed all might be lost, he touches once again on the opening motive, which now seems optimistic and grand. He does not want us to exit this movement despairing; hope springs forth, in the form of a . . .

IV. Finale ("Tema Russo")

Brace yourself! This is one wild movement, Russia by way of the Austro-Hungarian Empire—though you would not be able to suss this from the opening seconds of this movement, which sound like the orchestra re-tuning. Tchaikovsky calls for the instruments to be muted—the players literally attach bits of wood or plastic to their strings or insert plugs into the bells of their horns to dampen them—achieving an otherworldly, subdued sound. From this strange, attenuated sound, a series of held notes, a melody begins slowly to emerge, creeping out of its shell. Soon it gains momentum, learning to walk; then it grows a certain richness, a pellucid luster, which comes to a more solid-ground close; but, strangely (or not—this is the Tchaikovsky-verse), it wanes, failing as quickly as it birthed. A series of deceptive cadences, a musical device akin to a false ending, weakens the tune. It seems to beg for life, but is denied. Or is it?

Suddenly the wild rumpus begins. Tchaikovsky modulates to the work's home key of C major—finally!—and takes off running with an *allegro con spirito* (fast, full of life). The tune he writes—or quotes—is, as the title of the work suggests, very Russian, but more vivacious and buoyant, Tchaikovsky's homeland by way of Mozart's fertile melodic imagination. Listen to the tune (hard to miss): it comprises two principal building blocks: the head motive (eighth-notes) and the tail (sixteenth-notes), the concatenation of which, twice repeated, forms a single statement. Tchaikovsky is subtly referring to the opening of the first movement: not only is this music clearly in C major, but, like the opening bars, it commences with an unfinished chord. Things are beginning to come full circle; we are now officially nearing the long journey's end—though there is spirited merriment to be had before we part.

Just under two minutes into this short movement, things have begun to break down. A scuttling sixteenth-note motion derived from the tail of the tune supports the second statement. However, after propulsive buildup, Tchaikovsky arrives at a fuller, richer iteration of the "Tema Russo," after which the theme departs to the basses and cellos, as loud, full chords (a synthesis of both the accompaniment and the theme) play on the fiddles. A few seconds later, the composer backs off, changing the entire texture simply by incorporating eighth-note pizzicato, derived from the head of the melody. Now the basses and cellos grace the foreground, playing the melody with gusto—but they develop a tic at the end, as if they were stuck on the tail of the melody. Tchaikovsky uses the plucked strings, playing the notes G and B, to twist us into the depths of a peculiar new musical world, different and yet somehow akin to what preceded it. We could never have predicted it, yet it seems, once we hear it, not out of place.

Smoothly, using the pulsing, plucking eighth-notes to fashion his easy transition, Tchaikovsky now writes a gorgeous, lilting melody, played by the cellos, to contrast the juggernaut of the first tune—theme B. When this tune is repeated, he layers high violin commentary atop it. For the third statement of the new theme, Tchaikovsky is yet again up to his old motoric tricks, creating a countermelody that doubles as a pulse—substituting for the plucked strings, now enveloped into the texture. We are truly somewhere different. Soon, though, Tchaikovsky turns backward on a dime, dipping quickly into the "Tema Russo," our theme A, so that it not only returns, but regains its original glory in its original key.

But, of course, nothing is ever as it seems in the Tchaikovsky-verse, so immediately theme A takes a dark turn into what might be described as a roaming tonality. Without a point of reference—a tonal center, a home key—we have no home, akin to inherent musical anarchy where anything can happen because there are no governing laws. This wandering is brief, however, and eventually we land right in the center of a storm in the ear-bending key of C minor. But storms pass, and we come soon to somewhere calm, though now in the distant key of A-flat major. The tune is the niggling little "Tema Russo." After some more roaming, beneath which whizzing sixteenth-notes—the tail again— lend momentum, the music comes to a stop so pronounced that it could be the end of the piece—were it not in the key of E-flat major. After an apparently decisive cadence in this foreign key, the cellos are off and running again, with theme-B-derived violins above them. Tchaikovsky still has a few points to make about the synthesis of themes A and B. We hear a furtive little tune set high on the cello so that it sounds more like a mournful oboe or high bassoon. More roaming ensues, with rising melodic sequences contributing unbroken tension while the harmony drags behind. It is a method by which composers can quickly get among whichever keys they like, and the effect is dizzying and sets well as a contrast to the solidest of cadences.

Then something strange happens: though we have clearly landed on a tonic-sounding chord in D major, Tchaikovsky, unbeknownst to his listeners, has quietly changed the key in the score to C major. We are home but do not know it yet, and it is not until the pedal tone moments later that we are given any inkling of his intentions. In the meantime, heads and tails are dissected and tossed around pell-mell; chaos reigns. When we do get a full cadence, it is unsatisfying; unfinished business remains. Could it be the expansive fireworks that we've been waiting for—or is it the Russian hoedown? Tchaikovsky recapitulates theme A exactly, with one blemish that works to our advantage: it is easily, cleanly in C major. When theme B comes back, it too is in the home key. C major has exerted its will over all this music, and what was once staged in a distant foreign land has gone native, returned home.

Tchaikovsky writes a full heaving cadence, one that, existing as it does within the larger framework of the coda, could well have been the last moment of the piece—but the composer thwarts that with a quick series of descending chords, landing on a diminished seventh that pulls toward the dominant. Rather than simply ending the work here with a thump, Tchaikovsky executes the most glorious stunt, repeating, unblemished, the opening measures of the entire piece.. The effect is pure magic, as sweeping and grand as music gets. The choice is bold and unconventional, particularly for a work rooted so deeply in the music of his forebears: Schumann or Wagner might have played such a trick, but

Mozart or Haydn would have considered it too shocking to consider. He states this gorgeous, grand theme twice but does not linger, choosing instead to pick things up with reassertions of theme A, in the home key of C major, which leads us to the rollicking, splendid, totally prepared (and yet somehow surprising), thoroughly enchanting finish.

Nutcracker

"If ever Tchaikovsky wrote an ill-starred work," writes biographer Roland John Wiley, "it was *Nutcracker*. Had he known what miseries he would endure while writing it he would surely have refused; certainly when those miseries were acute he considered withdrawing his services from the project." It has brought him down to us through the ages—the piece is one of the most popular works ever penned—but was no fun while it was happening. "At the outset of the collaboration, however," continues Wiley, "prospects must have seemed bright."

In early 1890, the fifty-year-old composer was in particularly merry spirits, and why should he not have been? He was among the most famous composers in the world, with a surfeit of commissions ahead, a reputation, and no lack of ideas. His ballet *Sleeping Beauty* was an unqualified triumph, and for his coming work he was to collaborate with the same team, so success was all but assured. "Now," he wrote to his best friend, "dear Madame, you will ask me what I want to do. . . . If the good lord grants me life and good health, this will be an opera. . . . And then I must do another ballet (the one this season having had a great success)."

One of the reasons Tchaikovsky had such trouble getting his mind around *Nutcracker* was his distaste for the scenario. It was not something he chose, and he felt disconnected from the very strange material. "The subject of *Nutcracker*," wrote Modest Tchaikovsky, the composer's brother and amanuensis, "did not much please him." His dissatisfaction with the storyline coupled with rifts among the creative team did not create an easy working environment. Tchaikovsky threatened to withdraw—something the company could not suffer—but agreed to put aside his personal troubles, asking instead that the company postpone the work until the 1892-93 season.

The ballet originally was to be half of a double bill, coupled with a one-act opera to be called *King René's Daughter* (later called simply *Iolanta*). This commission had come from the state, from the directorate of imperial theaters, and was quite an honor—and also the reason the composer felt compelled to wrestle with a libretto he did not like, which was part of the deal. The story, based on a tale by E.T.A. Hoffmann, who was quite in vogue in Germany at the time, offers little in the way of stage action in the second act. The problems went deeper than that: the story, according to Wiley, "remains a simple children's tale, without significance as an allegory or parable; it is precisely what critics falsely accused *Sleeping Beauty* of being." From a strict perspective of the dance, he adds, "the leading characters do virtually no dancing, and the leading dancers have virtually no place in the story." Wiley finds other troubles besides. "The emphasis on mime in the first act," he writes, "gives way to *divertissement* in the second, thus making them seem more disconnected dramatically. That a ballet of this length should contain only one classical *pas* for the ballerina, and this near the end of the second act, was not lost on the critics." From this litany of troubles it becomes easy to understand Tchaikovsky's reluctance—and yet *Nutcracker* lives on, flawed, troubled, and critically panned, but one of the most performed pieces in the history of music.

The plot of *Nutcracker* is simple and strange, and one that, after being scaled down for the ballet, was deprived of much of the grimness in Hoffmann's version. A young German girl named Clara dreams that a nutcracker doll, given to her by her grandfather (Herr Drosselmeyer) at a family Christmas party, becomes a handsome prince who takes her to imaginary lands. It is there, in the Land of the Sweets, that her prince must do battle with the Mouse King—and together, victorious, Clara and the prince are presented with the gift of dances from many lands. The plot alone does little to explain the broad, worldwide success of this ballet: were Tchaikovsky not the composer, and were his music not completely innovative, exquisite, and beautifully enchanting, we would not know this piece today.

Note on the "Suite"

The score to a ballet, as opposed to a symphony or a concerto, is often not a freestanding musical entity suited to the concert platform. There may be portions that, though essential to the story or to the dance, are not inherently interesting as music in their own right. So often composers will concoct a suite, removing some of what they feel to be the duller moments ("musical wallpaper" is the cheeky term) and making a piece that can fly or flop based on its own musical coherence. Famous orchestral works that began life as ballets—Rimsky Korsakov's Scheherazade, *Stravinsky's* Petroushka, *and Ravel's* Daphnis and Chloe *to name a few—are refashioned suites. Do not therefore be surprised this Christmas, when you attend a danced performance of* The Nutcracker, *to find music you have not heard, even if you have explored the piece through this listening exercise. For those interested, there are plenty of recordings of the complete, unexpurgated score.*

I. "Miniature Overture"
CD I, Track 4

It's Christmas Eve at the home of Clara and Fritz (our heroine's bratty little brother), and their excited merriment brims from this overture. A stately, light-handed clip in brisk time (*allegro giusto*—"fast and strict") limns the festivities. The opening melody—theme A—which has antecedent and consequent phrases (the beginning and 0:05 respectively)—is repeated directly at 0:09, but shot through with some additional life: scurrying strings which, though they play a darling melody, are there primarily to activate the texture. The second tune—theme A1—at 0:18 is of a darker hue, cast in G minor, the "relative minor" of the home key of B-flat. The colors of the section are pure Tchaikovsky-verse: the winds do battle with the strings, trading blows, as if theme A were trying to reassert itself—perhaps standing for Fritz—during the mild torpor of theme A1. This leads not to a conflagration between them, but rather to a synthesis of both at 0:36, where Tchaikovsky uses the once agitated flutes to state theme A, strings buzzing beneath.

At 0:45 Tchaikovsky, under a long held tone in the oboe (which almost says "aha!" while acting on the listener like a magician's misdirection), extrapolates on the last bit of theme A, a mini-coda that serves as connective tissue to 0:49, where the sweet ascent of theme B is introduced. This little tune is as smooth and silken as theme A was jumpy and clipped, and we are now in F major, the dominant, a close key to which the composer modulates easily. He is not trying to shock us with incisive harmonic shifts, but rather trying to make us feel as at home as Clara and Fritz feel, a warm bed on a cold night. At 0:54, we hear theme B's consequent phrase, which is suspiciously like theme A1—confirmed at 1:02 when Tchaikovsky glances slightly at A1 before the second iteration of theme B, essentially the same though the latter has been beefed up slightly.

At 1:19, Tchaikovsky obsesses, spinning the last scrap of theme B to dizzying heights, taking us out of the realm of the sane and pure and placing us squarely in the center of a rush of ambiguity. This leads, after a wild, coda-like section at 1:26, to the inevitable restatement of theme A at 1:38, with theme A1 not long behind at 1:55. At 2:26, when Tchaikovsky repeats theme B, in the home key of B-flat major, we feel the movement coming quickly to a close, which it does soon there-after. There is nothing overly tricky about this section of *Nutcracker,* just good, clear, adorable music, designed to set the mood of comfort, hearth, home, and care. The final stroke is not too decisive; there is still a long way to go before Christmas morning.

II. "Danses Caractéristiques"

"Marche"
CD 1, Track 5

The boys, including Clara's mischievous brother Fritz, march into the room, illuminated by a splendid Christmas tree. The party has begun, and so has the ballet. This is a march, which means that the work is heard "in two" very clearly (strong-weak). Tchaikovsky marks the score tempo *di marcia viva* (brisk marching speed), meaning it is going to snap along. Like many of the short dances in this suite, the "Marche" consists of only one theme, run through a few times with only a brief transitional passage to offset it. In other words, what to listen for in this small section are not the trickeries of the form (there are none) or the contrast of melodies (there is only one), but what Tchaikovsky is able to do with such limited material. The theme is easily split into two discernable parts: triplets make up the head; the subsequent series of brief pickup notes that land clearly on the beat (called an *anacrusis*, and heard for the first time at 0:06) comprise the tail.

The first statement of the entire theme is presented obviously and unadorned, like a rhetorical statement in an argument. Notice how much Tchaikovsky makes out of the contrast between the head and tail of the tune just through cunning use of the orchestra. The former is scored for staid, stalwart horns without held tones to make it sound "wetter," while for the latter the composer artfully deploys the strings with bassoons playing a long, arching phrase beneath. These two elements join—along with the rest of the orchestra, including the remainder of the woodwinds and percussion—at the final chord crash at 0:12. The second statement is practically a note-for-note repeat, with one exception: the clarinets now replace bassoons in holding the long tones in the tail portion. This difference is subtle, one that you will really have to listen for, but it is not without import because the bassoons sounded reedy and insecure while the clarinets sound smoother and more sure. Tchaikovsky avails himself of this understated color change to push the countermelody to a higher register, preparing the coming orchestral thump.

At 0:25 we hear what sounds rhythmically like a restatement of the theme, but it is in a minor key, making it just different enough not be heard as a repeat but familiar enough not to be perceived as a wholly new theme. The tail is put through a similar transformation: the walking-bass-like sound that accompanied it before commutes upward in the string section—from the basses doubling cellos to the cellos doubling violas—while the chirping anacrusis figure, now in the winds, moves at a quicker pace. This new, vivified theme repeats once again, but while the head is exactly the same, the tail is changed to a cascade of notes scored for clarinets and bassoons (previously used primarily in the background) that leads us directly into two restatements of the original theme in its original key, completely unchanged.

At 1:02, the theme catches fire. An antiphonal scamper between the winds and the strings gives us a slight break from the opening material (anything might get wearisome after six repeats). Tchaikovsky uses this connective chunk to fashion momentum; between high-flying flutes and swelling horns, the composer appears to be leading us somewhere both majestic and threatening. Once this sort of thrust is initiated, especially in the middle of such a short section, it cannot be easily repealed, so when the theme returns at 1:15, Tchaikovsky has whipped the motion into a spectacular swishing orchestral wave. In a gesture Wagner would have proudly called his own, the strings and winds join forces to create a swirling hurricane, scraps of which are passed around the entire orchestra (with the exception of the brass, who play the theme). Imagine this live: it would come off as positively quadraphonic. The transformation of the tail is equally enchanting: Tchaikovsky bids the horns, once the hearkeners of chaos, to join the bassoons and clarinets in long tones beneath the anacrusis. This new casting of the theme follows at 1:28, pursued by a direct restatement of its minor version at 1:41. Finally, at 1:53, we hear the theme in its newly emboldened version one last time, and with this, the short-but-potent work draws to a quick, unceremonious close.

"Danse de la Fée-Dragée" ("Dance of the Sugar Plum Fairies")
CD 1, Track 6

It's magic time. This dance is one of the most famous pieces of music ever written, suffering commercial exploitation (including, alas, disco or techno remixes to augment televised jewelry advertisements) every Christmas. It earned Tchaikovsky his deserved reputation as an accomplished fantasist; the colors alone are a masterstroke of imagination, let alone the memorable melody. This section—one of the first dances in the Land of the Sweets, the dreamland where Clara is taken after her Nutcracker prince defeats the Mouse King—is as delicate and queer as the prior movement was grand and full of expansive aplomb. The dance begins quietly in G minor, with subdued pizzicato strings trading beats and offbeats among themselves, a Russian "oom-chuck." To create this sense of distant fairyland, Tchaikovsky uses a then-new instrument called a celesta (for the first time in history) to play the theme—theme A—and a bass clarinet (a larger, lower, incarnation of the instrument) to play the accompanying countermelodic cascade. The result is bizarre, straight out of another world: we have left the orchestra and traveled to an outlandish place where anything can happen. E.T.A. Hoffmann would have been impressed.

Like all perfect melodies, theme A begins with a head, followed, at 0:17, by a tail. Listen, in the latter, to how the creaky low clarinet pushes downward while the high, sprite-like celesta blinks about. The first half repeats at 0:25, but when, at 0:32, we expect to hear the tail, what we get is almost but not quite. Tchaikovsky does give us the tail, but in an unexpected incarnation, thickening the texture, adding woodwinds and passing the countermelody to the clarinets. This first portion wraps up neatly at 0:40 with a decisive cadence, dovetailing into a new theme—theme B.

Where the first theme, both head and tail, is favored by the smart snaps of pizzicato strings, theme B is comparatively lugubrious, full of long held notes, the instruments no longer plucked but bowed. The celesta, its capacity to shock exhausted, now sinks into the texture. The key is B major, the dominant of the home key of E minor; celesta aside, this is shaping up to be a straightforward movement.

At 1:03, Tchaikovsky shuffles off the quotidian exercise of themes and cadences, composing a quasi-cadenza (the portion of a concerto where the soloist plays unaccompanied, often a show of technical prowess) for the celesta. It is almost as if the instrument, which is not the star of this piece—this is no Concerto for Celesta—has her diva moment, reminding us she is still worthy of attention, and, at 1:12, it is through the timeless riffing that Tchaikovsky plops us back to theme A, aided by the capitulating winds. The now familiar melody is given extra heft by dint of its new orchestral cloaking: chugging bowed strings replace earlier pizzicatos. Quickly, almost cruelly, Tchaikovsky brings the Fairies' dance to a sudden (but satisfying) finish.

"Danse Russe Trépak" ("Russian Dance: Trépak")
CD I, Track 7

Yet another in the vast selection of Tchaikovsky's enduring chestnuts, another theme you have certainly heard before, this spirited dance stands as emblematic of the Yuletide season. Preening and posing with vainglorious gusto, the Russian dancers in the Land of the Sweets angle to impress Clara and her prince with their shameless display. It is a fast, furious minute of pure Slavic bluster. Like the "Marche," this short movement is built on one theme, often repeated, with a brief transitional passage thrown in to create contrast. The lone melody commences with a head and concludes, at 0:03, with a tail—but before there is any hint of a melody, the movement opens with a majestic (but somehow chirpy and bright) crash. Tchaikovsky achieves this effect—a chord that is loud but not overbearing—by avoiding the high screechy registers of each of his instruments, and omitting the horns (which would tip the decibels) altogether. The effect is forthright but not overwhelming.

The melody, head and tail alike, repeats without any variation both at 0:06 and at 0:13. During the third iteration, Tchaikovsky ups the ante, pushing the flute to a higher and therefore more audible register (lending to the proceedings a more caffeinated quality), adding a lightly tapped tambourine. Using this slightly altered orchestration to perk our ears a little, Tchaikovsky then changes things altogether, moving, at 0:25, into his transitional material, flipping the texture so that the instruments that once assayed the melody (winds and high strings) now move to the background as the low strings are now deployed to assert the material of the foreground. And at 0:37, Tchaikovsky writes a second transitional theme, a bold maneuver, leading us, perhaps, to believe, that this dance will take off to all manner of fanciful places. Fortunately, it does not: at 0:43 we are back—and buzzing with brio. Tchaikovsky deploys the entire orchestra to the last instrument, imbuing this final push to the end with overwhelming, high-volume vigor. And, at 0:54, Tchaikovsky spins the tail into a furor, not so much ending as slamming hard on the brakes.

"Danse Arabe" ("Arabian Dance")
CD I, Track 8

It is time now for a whiff of exotica by way of the Western World. For artists in the Victorian era, the Far East held an endless fascination, and this was especially true for the Russians. Members of the so-called "Mighty Five," that coterie of major Russian composers (whose acceptance Tchaikovsky longed for), frequently turned to the sexy sounds of the far-off Arab lands—impressions all drawn from *The Arabian Nights:* think Rimsky-Korsakov's *Scheherazade*—so it stands to reason that Tchaikovsky would include some in this portion of *Nutcracker,* his own index of exotica.

Eastern music often uses a *drone* (a drawn-out sound in the bass that never departs), so Tchaikovsky uses this technique to create his fantastic Arab mood. At the beginning, basses and cellos pulsate insistently (this constantly repeated pattern is referred to not only as a drone but also as an ostinato), setting the mood, creating a sonic pasha's carpet above which a retinue of winds, led by the newly introduced English horn (a darker, hoarser oboe), lay out their alluring tune at 0:07. This is not so much a proper theme—though for the sake of clarity let's call it theme A—as it is a gesture, a mood, whose most important musical nugget is the sexy slither of the clarinet at 0:11. The whole dance is drawn from this single kernel.

After Tchaikovsky repeats the whole of theme A, he introduces its complement, theme B, at 0:22. The first tune is rooted in downward motion, so for contrast this new theme moves upward. Scored for strings, it has a warmer hue. At 0:33, Tchaikovsky uses a single, exposed tambourine to great exotic effect, separating the two iterations of theme B with a decisive, percussive stroke, eventually leading us back to a recapitulation of theme A at 0:54. All the while, he never stops that insistent ostinato in the basses and cellos but, because it has been going on for so long, it is easy to be lulled into forgetting it is there.

The repeat of theme A is almost exact, save that now the bassoons lead the melodic charge and the tambourine persists. And when theme B returns at 1:09, it too has been altered imperceptibly (but dramatically): the melody is actually pitched higher, and, like the tambourine, the bassoons have not been dropped, but now play a juicy inner melody running in contrary motion to the tune. This makes it difficult to say whether theme B, in this particular casting, is moving up or down—a fantastical bit of musical *trompe l'oeil*. The composer is amassing his forces above the drone: once a color is introduced, Tchaikovsky tends not to drop it. Slow, quiet insistence is the name of this particular musical game.

At 1:38, at the end of this new theme B, Tchaikovsky slides gracefully from a major chord to a minor chord while the tambourine taps again beneath. It is a moment that could have been composed by Mahler; we question, for that second, in which key we are. On the one hand, the drone tells our ear that we have never left the home key—or even the home chord—but at this slippery moment, Tchaikovsky toys with our sense of musical place. When the drone changes color at 1:42 around the final statement of both themes, you might well not hear it, largely because you have become so accustomed to its presence that it now lives in your subconscious; but also because, while the same notes are being played by the string section, the instruments have changed. The basses now hold an open fifth interval while the cellos and violins trade off rhythmic beats and offbeats. It gives the drone a little shiver, and lends it a fuller sound, even if the main impact is subliminal. When Tchaikovsky repeats theme B at 1:57, he does so beneath a high, wailing solo oboe playing a snake charmer's exhortation. At 2:07, cascading winds respond to its call. At 2:11, the bassoon takes over for the oboe, and at 2:24, the call is passed to the clarinet (in its lowest, *chalumeau*, register). The movement concludes with a quick cycling through of all the various musical characters we have met during this short journey to Arabia—and the opening cello ostinato is back to see us collectively through to the end.

"Danse Chinoise" ("Chinese Dance")
CD I, Track 9

Yet another enchanting work you have probably heard many times, especially around the holidays—and another glance at the East, at the exotica of far-off lands. Like many other *Nutcracker* dances, it is based on a single theme—doubly so, here, because as the movement is so short there is not even time for it to be offset by the usual transitional material. It starts with low, guffawing bassoons blurting away—another ostinato figure, redolent of the "Danse Arabe." Like the preceding movement, the drone never strays from a single pitch: B-flat, the tonic note. This creakiness (it is an in-joke among musicians to call the bassoon a "farting bedpost") is soon offset by a lissome, graceful, bird-like melody in the flutes, a tune you will recognize. This flute statement forms the question to which pizzicato strings, trading beats and off-beat, will answer at 0:08. Tchaikovsky repeats this entire exchange once before building on it. Then, at 0:22, after a pealing of flutes (now doubled by the piccolo, which sounds a full octave higher), once again the theme repeats, albeit in a slightly more elaborate version, still scored for flutes which remain doubled—and where a question comes an answer will follow, once again from the plucked strings. And again Tchaikovsky repeats the entire new(ish) passage.

At 0:39, the theme is repeated, now gifted with a grander, fuller texture beneath it. Tchaikovsky not only introduces the exotic percussive ping of a glockenspiel (more Chinoiserie than authentic Chinese, but it does make its point) but also thickens the mix with clarinets playing quick, quiet figures that run up and down the notes of the chords (called an *arpeggio*). We hear the theme again, in its original incarnation. By the time we reach 0:56, Tchaikovsky is already beginning his push to the end: edgy flutes drive this short movement to a rapid climax.

"Danse des Mirlitons" ("Dance of the Red Pipes")
CD 1, Track 10

The sound of the flutes Tchaikovsky assigns to play the tune of this movement has since become a proper noun: Nutcracker Flutes. Over a light pizzicato string accompaniment, he composes another in a long line of utterly memorable melodies—theme A. These flutes serve as the watchword of this dance, and their texture—many playing as one, a sort of superflute—is of equal importance to their material. As always, Tchaikovsky repeats the tune twice, but while doing so prepares you for something that is to come: listen, at 0:11, for a subtle (but exquisite) countermelody in the bassoon. This serves not only to buoy the harmony but to dazzle our ear on simultaneous levels, an augur of something more yet to come. At 0:34, when the flutes, once the principal melodic force, take a more textural role, the counter-melody—which is passed from English horn to bass clarinet—moves from background to foreground. It is not so much a wholly new theme as a transition, for at 0:46, following a gorgeous cascade of strings (taking their cue from the flute filigree), theme A returns, along with its attendant countermelody—which has evolved slightly. It is no longer a subliminal presence beneath the melody; it has developed into a full-blown secondary theme, shot through the entire string section, earnestly chugging away beneath the famous Nutcracker Flutes.

At 1:13, when what is now the fourth statement of theme A draws to a close, Tchaikovsky envelops his final cadence with warm horns, to aid (or so we are to believe) in bringing this statement to a more deci-sive close. But he has a more brutal use for them in mind: they seem to wrest the texture wholly from the chattiness of the flutes and strings, twisting the piece quickly from a light divertimento to a mad Slavic dance—theme B—which is a fantastical choice. To make this radical departure even more pronounced—and stranger—the modulation from the key of D major to A minor is a surprising and piquant turn. At 1:30, when the strings join the fray, they do not portend frivolity or lightness—or do they? As quickly as Tchaikovsky used the proto-mini-malist exertions of theme B to appropriate the mood from the flutes, they deftly reclaim the proceedings at 1:46, picking up where theme B leaves off and dovetailing immediately into a rededicated principal motive, theme A. After two restatements, countermelody and all, the piece smashes shut.

III. "Valse des Fleurs" ("Waltz of the Flowers")
CD I, Track II

Nutcracker outlines a grand, sweeping tour of exotic lands (or what was then exotic to a Muscovite). We have been to the Orient, to deepest

Arabia, and to the Land of the Sweets, a magical if unsettling place within the darkest reaches of the imagination of E.T.A. Hoffmann by way of the madly original Tchaikovsky. Now, gentle listeners, it seems time to settle in for a rousing close in that least (yet somehow most) far-off realm: Vienna, where genteel waltzes and madness blithely co-exist. For a composer working in the latter part of the nineteenth century, a waltz was emblematic of the (soon-to-collapse) Hapsburg Empire, which would be commemorated only some two decades hence in composer Maurice Ravel's final musical essay on the topic, *La Valse*. In that work the Frenchman pushes the form, with its insistent, insouciant "in three" pattern, to a terrifying, *Red Shoes*-like climax, the overwhelming sound of waning gentility. Once you have waltzed with Ravel, you can never dance again. Innocence dies on the vine as the nineteenth century gives way to the twentieth; *fin de siècle* propriety collapses into obscurity. Ravel was hardly working in a sui generis vacuum; he took his cues from the final moments of *Nutcracker*.

Waltzes, in their purest form, are made up of two themes—A and B—which, in a way, form an antecedent and consequent of one another. In other words, A begs a question, B answers. Tchaikovsky does not disappoint on this formal front, but with his trademark neurotic insistence, he shakes the form, so that the "Valse des Fleurs" has within it two discernable levels: the sublimely wistful and beautiful, beneath which lurks a certain amount of borderline-murderous terror.

To begin, Tchaikovsky uses a grand introduction, wiping away from our aural minds all of the more rhythmically regulated music that came before. Horns outline an expansive theme in D major; if we are yet to call this, in our minds, a real theme or simply to bask in the warmth of a free-flowing, high-climbing overture, we do not know. When, at 0:19, Tchaikovsky introduces the solo harp for the first time in the entire work and allows it to (apparently) extemporize an unconstrained cadenza, where things will land is anybody's guess. His orchestral thrift, saving the harp until this one last moment, is certainly admirable. However, as our ears are lulled into complacency, expecting a series of sugary harp flights, Tchaikovsky, at 0:57, launches into the genuine oom-pah-pah of the waltz. Horns, working together as a single instrument, play the haughty theme from the introduction at

1:01. Theme A has been with us all along, and at 1:09, a nervous solo clarinet—theme A1—answers. This entire section is presented twice without frippery. At 1:34, following a grand swelling pickup from the strings (another anacrusis—recall the opening "Marche"), the hauteur of theme B is presented for the first time. For this occasion, Tchaikovsky composes one of his simplest yet most engaging melodies, a soaring answer to the subdued question of the principal theme. This, too, is presented twice. (Listen within the confines of the theme, and you will hear the Nutcracker Flutes from the previous movement as a response.) These two themes are both complementary and contrasting. They are in the same key (an uncommon move) and both are arguments for the waltz (as opposed to working against it), but where theme A is calm, baleful, favored by more muted forces, theme B is exposed, soaring, built around warm strings.

At 2:07, theme A re-emerges from the sweep of theme B—though, as is common in the Tchaikovsky-verse, not exactly: flutes—Nutcracker Flutes—respond, as if bits of both themes A1 and B have bled through, only to be completely wiped out at 2:39 by theme B in its original form. To follow, lest we tire of this back-and-forth between themes A and B, at 3:10 Tchaikovsky spins out some new material—theme B1—which, though audibly related to theme B, has a character all its own. It is almost a synthesis between the two principal motives: it has the rhythmic implications of theme B in the melody (played by flutes, reminiscent of the twittering response in theme B), but the pulled-back character of A, and in its accompaniment are darting strings reminiscent of theme A1. For the second iteration of theme B1, Tchaikovsky deploys a triangle, making clear with this one deft, subtle touch that we are somewhere new.

He pushes us to a bleaker place at 3:41, with even newer material—theme B2—played by the ominously hued violas and cellos, answered by slight, pensive violin figures that become even more pronounced at 3:57, a second iteration of B2. It is as if we are barely hanging on to the bright memory of theme B as a cloud passes over it. But in the Tchaikovsky-verse all that is good and light triumphs over darkness . . . sometimes . . . so at 4:12 theme B1 returns, colored by flowing woodwinds, working itself into a frenzy of echolalia at

4:27. This trick—the act of pushing something to an extreme, while working a sleight of hand beneath it—leads us uneasily (but clearly) at 4:34 back to theme A, done slightly differently, of course, through the subtleties of orchestration. As might be expected by now, at 5:04 theme B follows—twice—little changed, grand as ever. This in turn is what Tchaikovsky uses to marshal some serious momentum, creating, at 5:33, a theme A explosion. Tchaikovsky calls for the entire orchestra to force this moment, pushing hard toward the end of the movement—and of *Nutcracker*. The composer has been saving this fire; even when he pulls back slightly, at 5:41, you can still feel the push of the final cadence: 5:51 feels like the windup, 5:56 the punch, and 6:12 the final collapsing stroke—the coda. All of this final movement's themes are accounted for, and as we have been in the home key for pages now, there is little question as to the finality of this passage. It has become, through compositional oomph, an unstoppable juggernaut, ejecting us, with a series of huge, demanding final hits, back into the quotidian world. The land of the sweets now lies sadly behind us.

Symphony No. 6 ("Pathetique")

CD 2, Tracks 4–5 (Movements I and IV)

I am prouder of this symphony than of any other of my compositions.

—Tchaikovsky

To discuss the music of Tchaikovsky and omit discussion of turmoil, fire, inner longing, *cri de coeur*, and inspiration is to miss the point, and this is never more true than in an attempt to understand his sixth—and final—symphony. As overblown and even downright annoying as these notions can get when discussing classical music, and as deftly as they evade any exactness, when trying to get a toehold on the music of Tchaikovsky, not only are they relevant, they are absolute. One must not only dip into his work but into his life, because, for this composer, they are inseparable. "I literally cannot live without working," he wrote, "for as soon as one piece of work is finished and one would wish to relax, instead of resting, i.e. abandoning oneself to the pleasures of the weary toiler who has earned the right to the alluring *dolce far niente,* one is a prey to depression and melancholy, to thoughts of the futility of earthly existence, fear for the future, fruitless regrets about the irretrievable past, the meaning of earthly existence, in a word, all that which poisons the life of a man who is not engrossed in work and inclined to hypochondria, and the result is the desire to tackle some new work without delay." It is from this neurasthenic anima that Tchaikovsky's final symphony is wrought.

"There is no structure," writes Tchaikovsky scholar Timothy L. Jackson, "without ideology." In other words, without understanding the artists' life and creed, we cannot begin to get a window into their work. "Thus," Jackson continues, "the belief that one can study 'pure' structure, divorced from considerations of the structure's attendant ideology, seems misplaced." To know the work is to know the man, and vice versa.

It is the construction of this work—its formal design, or lack thereof—that is the most controversial. According to some of his critics, the peculiar overarching shape of the "Pathétique" betrays Tchaikovsky's inability to create a satisfying symphonic structure on the models of Haydn, Mozart, or Beethoven. But one man's discontinuity is another man's raw emotional statement, so it is in the very oddness of this work—a symphony that both plays at and balks symphonic conventions—that the true emotional gist lies. "There will still be much that is new in the form of this work," wrote Tchaikovsky.

There is something prophetic about a composer's final work, especially within the symphonic genre—which for composers is the greatest paradigmatic consummation of musical thought (even more so than opera because it is pure music, no plot or text required). But did Beethoven, Bruckner, or Mahler (despite his half-completed Tenth) know that their ninth symphonies would be their last? The sheer amounts of mystical prophecy accorded parting works are valued insights, from the perspective of posterity, which always casts a keener eye than an in-the-moment response. In the case of Tchaikovsky's controversial demise—perhaps he was forced into suicide by the state rather than admit his homosexuality—his final utterance bears some examination as a goodbye because it is as likely as not that he knew—either in his mind or heart—that this work would be among his last. The symphony is as emotionally fraught, brooding, and death-conscious a work as he ever wrote, phantasmagoric in its emotional and musical scope, at turns profound and grotesque, ironic and fiercely bitter—as was his life.

There is a program, or story, to the work, but we do not know what exactly it is. Unlike the symphonies of Berlioz, the composer who all but invented the symphony-as-storytelling technique called program music—this has no libretto. Tchaikovsky's Sixth bears a secret story.

"While on my travels," the composer wrote in February 1893, "I had an idea for another symphony—a program work this time, but its program will remain a mystery to everyone—let them guess." Guess they have: in the course of musical history, much ink has been spilled after the composer's invitation to consider, but there is no official answer. There is even speculation about the moniker "Pathétique" (which means not "pathetic," but rather "of pathos," or "that which arouses our sympathetic sadness and compassion"): did the composer want it, or did his brother (and biographer) Modest add it *post facto*. Today, over a century later, we are still guessing. "This program," according to the composer, "is imbued with subjectivity. During my journey, while composing it in my thoughts, I often wept a great deal." That is all you have to go on—the story, such as it is, is devastatingly sad.

Originally, it was intended to be a "life" symphony, full, Tchaikovsky said, of "death," "collapse," and "disappointment." Yet the music he found himself writing was cheerful, robust, affirming—and in the key of E-flat major, the "heroic" key (of Beethoven's "Eroica" Symphony and the opening glittering cascade in Wagner's *Ring* cycle). Could this music, eventually scrapped, labeled as sketches for an aborted seventh symphony, really have been attached to the "life" program over which he wept? Alexander Poznansky, Tchaikovsky's psychobiographer, asks this question: "If the Sixth Symphony was intended to be somehow autobiographical, why, then, was it so pervasively tragic in tone? No truly catastrophic events accompanied his final years. He was at the peak of his creative powers, famous, and loved by those whom he loved." Perhaps outer appearances masked his inner turmoil, á la Richard Cory, the figure in the E.A. Robinson poem who had it all yet put a bullet through his head. The best way to think of the work is not as the composer's autobiography, but as his own attempt at psychobiography.

Tchaikovsky was in love with Bob Diadov, a love that dared not speak its name in the late 1800s—the famously repressive Victorian era—a love that was assiduously denied by friends and family after the composer's death. Perhaps convention got the better of him. Whatever the answer, the Sixth Symphony not only still compels but keeps us guessing. "A biographer incautious enough to believe he has seen Tchaikovsky plain," writes the brilliant scholar Richard Taruskin, author of the masterpiece *Defining Russia Musically,* "has only gazed credulously upon a construction of his own making, reflecting (like all "others") the writer's projected sense of himself."

When Tchaikovsky finally set to work in earnest on the Sixth Symphony, he wrote quickly, composing it in less than two months, and taking another month to complete the orchestration. In October 1893, after it was complete, he made revisions, and prepared a two-piano version, which was standard marketing practice at the time—cultivated persons would buy these arrangements to perform in their living rooms or at salons. In that era, it was how people became familiar with the newest music, commercial recordings being still in the future. On 20 October, there was a reading of this reduction—with a young unknown composer/pianist by the name of Serge Rachmaninoff in attendance—and the premiere, among the hotly anticipated highlights of the season, was given in St. Petersburg on 28 October 1893, with the composer conducting.

The symphony did not enter the world easily. "I must confess," wrote observer Jules Konyus, who was present at the two-piano reading, "that I was not in the least attracted by the actual music of the Sixth Symphony since the author's performance was as bad as one may imagine. His red hands with thick and by no means supple fingers pounded out the most poignant passages crudely and hurriedly, as if this hastened to finish and rid themselves." Another present wrote: "The symphony did not make much impression." The actual premiere of the fully scored version was hardly a success, with an audience reaction that ran from ambivalent to hostile.

Then, a few days later, the composer died in a shroud of mystery— after which, at its subsequent second performance, the "Pathétique" was declared a masterpiece. "Perhaps," writes Jackson, "the work's content had been made acceptable by the composer's death, once it was suspected that, unable to bear his homosexuality any longer, he had committed suicide. In other words, only when Tchaikovsky could be comfortably pegged as an '*un*happy' homosexual, and the 'Pathétique' interpreted as a self-indictment (i.e. as his own pronouncement through his music that the 'right' and 'proper' solution to his 'homosexual problem' was suicide)—only then could the 'Pathétique' become morally acceptable." His death washed away sin, and therefore his Sixth Symphony, a de facto last will and testament, served for the narrow-minded Russian audience as a confession, a step on the road to perdition, absolution, redemption, and a return to the grace that only death can provide.

I: Adagio—Allegro non troppo
CD 2, Track 4

The piece begins with pure, subliminal agitation. It is marked *adagio* (slow), a tempo usually reserved for the second movement in a standard sonata-allegro symphonic opening. Merely by commencing at this tempo, Tchaikovsky states (rather bluntly) that he is going to do something completely outside the confines of expectation —and he does not disappoint. There is also the matter of key: a work with a home key (tonic) of B-minor should begin in B-minor, but the "Pathétique" does not. Instead, it starts in E-minor—a full fourth away—and descends to the home key, landing there rather restlessly. A bass line, which creeps downward in what is called a *descending chromatic*, is a sort of classical music in-joke, a clear and incontestable symbol of death, to which Tchaikovsky's audience would have been privy. This notion comes, originally, from "Dido's Lament" in Henry Purcell's opera *Dido and Aeneas*, with the same pendulous descent laying the foundation for the words "When I am laid in earth." Tchaikovsky certainly knew this, and used it to set the mood: it is all about death. This is abetted by his assigning this opening melody—the "death" theme—to slithering bassoons over husky cellos and basses. This tune emerges from a swampy murk, a long, dark night of the soul; it sounds furtive and desperate, irresolute and strange. Listen to the actual rhythm of the musical scrap (one hesitates to call this creaking a melody): "da-da-DA-dum." Two notes form a pickup, on a weak beat (another anacrusis), which then moves to an uncertain note on the subsequent strong beat. This in turn resolves, but again on a weak beat, stealing its thunder. The focus of the phrase is not on the resolution but on the tension that precedes it. From this conceptual kernel Tchaikovsky derives the entire movement.

A repeat of death follows a long, pregnant pause—intentionally reminiscent of Wagner's prelude to *Tristan und Isolde*. The melody takes a few more turns, arriving, once again at a suspended non-resolution at 1:50, another *Tristan* homage, with the foregoing passage permeated by the dark herald of a solo horn playing a dissonance that never quite resolves. This is the end of the short-lived Adagio portion, a brief flicker of an opening paragraph, which sloughs off into another freighted pause.

From 1:55 the movement takes off, ricocheting instantly (albeit quietly) from moony silence to slingshot allegro. Tchaikovsky has taken death and sped it up, shoving the same notes into a fraction of the time (called a *diminution*). The melody—"death creeps"—is fleet but by no means jubilant, made up of two characteristic portions from which Tchaikovsky will construct the entire movement: the head motive ("death sped up") and the tail motive (fast, fleet-footed sixteenth-notes scampering above offbeat chords). At this point, one iteration of "death creeps" is followed by another, each having a slight discoloration. This spins, at around 2:10, into an elaboration of the tail that spirals downward, at 2:19, into a surging version of "death creeps," cellos pulsing beneath a heavy string recasting. Tchaikovsky then bids us rise with portent, soaring to a high F-sharp (which is not coincidentally the pitch of the dissonant horn in the Adagio) at 2:38. This makes the low throb of the basses and cellos, which are added to the texture at 2:40, seem gruffer by contrast, vacant, a growl from below.

After Tchaikovsky pushes things earthward, at 2:48 he invents a variation on death favored by a veneer of ebullience—"death prances." It feels lightheaded, slightly joyful, like a salve, and is derived from the rhythm of death. At 3:05 he switches to the tail of "death creeps," which surges forward, gathering momentum and orchestral strength until, at 3:45, Tchaikovsky marks his score *un poco animado* (a little animated) and the movement reaches a fevered pitch, apocalyptic brass blaring their own version of death. This augurs even more fire: Tchaikovsky twists the score into full-throttle orchestral climax, flaring and soaring, taking up where the brass left off. But he will not overwhelm us with power . . . not yet; by 4:03 he begins a retreat, as if the clockworks of his symphony are winding down. By 4:12, what was once a mighty yell fizzles to one lamentable cello sawing away, and even this cannot hold: by 4:39, after even more dwindling, a solo viola protests into another weighty silence.

We can almost hear the composer, phoenix-like, picking himself up at 4:43, dusting himself off, trying to hold on with the idea that good will prevail. To depict this, he invents one of his most soaring, humid themes—"life"—the foil to death. Where the previous theme moves upward in a minor key, this one cascades lovingly downward in the relative major. Where the former was full of short phrases betwixt pauses, this melody is long, arching, and languorous. Listen carefully, because in the middle of the texture, almost imperceptible, are the horns playing their once dissonant F-sharp in exactly the same register as they did before. This is intentional: the grim specter of death lurks beneath all this melodic joy.

Once Tchaikovsky has given us a few moments to languish in the beauty of life, allowing us to feel emboldened, refreshed, as if we can safely carry on, surprisingly he moves on to a third theme—"optimism." This tune rises lyrically but cautiously above a hoofbeat-like repeated figure (an ostinato), trading back and forth between the flute and bassoon, the soprano and bass of the woodwind choir. Symphonies are supposed to have two themes only, so this new development would have caused a twitter amongst polite attendees in Victorian-era Moscow. What were cultivated ears supposed to make of this diversion? The tendency of the melody is a refreshed can-do spirit, but there is grimness lurking beneath it: the strings hammer away quietly at the same F-sharp in the same register as our prior wraith-like horn. This would be lost on anyone save those with the sharpest of ears, but it subliminally reminds the listener that no matter where he might take us, the truth of this work is unavoidable: death is never far from Tchaikovsky's mind.

At 5:46 begins a complementary theme to optimism, redolent of life in that it moves downward in a grand fashion—but the forward thrust of the ostinato remains, so it reads more like an answer to the question posed by optimism than like a wholly new theme. When Tchaikovsky repeats this slightly new material, one detail does fascinate: the F-sharp has now dropped an octave, a deportee from violin to viola, just as it did in the opening Adagio. When, at 6:31, there is a third iteration of optimism, Tchaikovsky employs many more instruments and takes the whole tune up a step.

By 6:58, the motion, which threatens to turn into a full-scale martial march, abates into silence, followed by a creaky rendering of life, stretched out (called an *augmentation*), nakedly exposed without the ballast of its harmony and the expressive heavy vibrato of the strings to shield it. Listen for the ominous shading of chromatic descent. This too bleeds into a laden silence. Then Tchaikovsky once again rehearses the life theme, spinning the triplets from optimism into an accompaniment beneath them, going so far as to completely change the meter from a duple (where each beat is divided into two sub-beats) to a triple (each beat containing three). It gives the moment an erotic heft, an undulating thrust. Life lives.

In the words of Yeats, "Things fall apart / the center cannot hold," which is exactly what happens to life at 8:17. Everything seemed to be going so well—too well—and so things begin their inevitable breakdown. Herein lies the tragedy, because the movement could easily have ended here, glowing, hopeful, death easily conquered. But things simply do not work that way in the Tchaikovsky-verse. So from glee Tchaikovsky descends, using the dotted off-rhythm of the last two notes of life—sad echolalia—to push downward until, at 9:08, a solo clarinet furtively assays life, a waif in contrast to the soaring strings in which this melody was so recently cast. In the barren moment when life sloughs from the lowest reaches of the clarinet's register to the bassoon—marked *quintuple piano*, the quietest moment in the entirety of Tchaikovsky's oeuvre—all seems utterly and devastatingly lost. Life, once vivid and prosperous, is snuffed.

Fight remains. Before explaining the coming storm—and it *is* coming—an explanation as to what makes this next moment so shocking is in order. Certainly the volume: things move from *quintuple piano* (pianisisisisimo*)* to *double forte*, a slow fade to a loud jolt, but something else is afoot: the key. For nearly ten minutes, over half the movement, there has not been a single modulation since the introduction of "death creeps." In fact, the opposite has been true: the bulk of the first half is predicated on *not* moving, on staying inside the same key. So even when a theme like life or optimism emerged from the thanatophilic fray, there was still a niggling foreboding that death was always with us in some nascent form. Now, in a sudden Hadean flash, Tchaikovsky runs roughshod over everything he has set up, not only jolting us with an orchestral hit that Stravinsky would have penned proudly, but crashing, without any preparation, into the key of C minor. This modulation to the most intrusive, dissonant key possible would have sent more than one member of the subscription audience running for the exit. It happens in a flash, but in the Tchaikovsky-verse there are always dire musical consequences for rash actions.

What ensues next is no less than a herald of apocalypse. Crunches over a throbbing bass—which, as foretold in the Adagio portion, descends chromatically—push and pull, vaguely familiar yet somehow un-placeable in our lexicon of this movement's melodies. At 10:15 our worst fears are confirmed: "death creeps" returns, redoubled. Over a scurrying frantic *fugato* (a quasi-fugue) this terrifying tune lurches, prowls, and bites as Tchaikovsky twists both the head and tail into his violent witches' brew. "Death prances" is also there, defaced, another demoniac character in the Stygian morass. And, at 10:47, an unthinkable tragedy occurs: what was once the tail of life has been brutally morphed into a despotic bleating fury in the trumpet. Death has completely consumed life. But when things look their blackest, even Tchaikovsky cannot sustain this animal fury. At 11:01, the music begins to dissipate, so that by 11:07 all that remains of the tragedy is guttural growling from the basses and cellos. A cinematic surging in the horns (in this era before cinema) is an attempt at another burst of furious anger, but this too subsides to a lone horn—not playing the F-sharp, mercifully—at 11:58.

At 12:00, a new rendering of "death creeps" slips onto the stage, with a destination note of the menacing F-sharp in the same register. Tchaikovsky is forcing us to survey the vast devastation of all he has wrought while death—or, in this case, "death creeps"—dances about mockingly, a chilling musical landscape. As we breathe it in, death's dance grows more bacchanalian with every passing second until, at 12:27, "death creeps" evolves into a truly wicked orchestral declamation. When, at 12:34, Tchaikovsky bounces the melody antiphonally between the strings and the winds, with brass as ballast, it almost seems to be seeking consent from the rest of the orchestra, gaining power and potency. At 13:01, tragedy strikes again: another high-decibel "death creeps," involving the entire orchestra, acquires even more might from another source, the swelling accompaniment triplets from optimism. Like life before it, optimism has been devoured. This is confirmed at 13:09 when that motive's second half is played by the trumpets, shades of what happened to the tail of life earlier.

Of course, this is still the Tchaikovsky-verse, and what goes up must inevitably come down. This fire fades, looping and seething its way downward, until, at 13:27, it remains a soupy low-register shell—all on a pedal point of F-sharp, that still ominous pitch. Could it be that this note, so threatening throughout, is a double agent that might well prove to be our secret hero? At the moment it seems either to have stopped death in its tracks—or maybe it is yet another grim manifestation. Regardless of the musical consequences, the moment is electrifying. Tchaikovsky creates a rigid swamp out of which, at 13:53, climbs life, clawing its way up from the muddle, screaming to be heard. It is perhaps the most stunning moment in the piece, the moment Tchaikovsky indicates we might make it out of this symphony alive. Death still lurks in the form of an F-sharp pedal throughout, but all is not lost. Scraps of life echo in the low horns, bleating, gasping for breath; the struggle is not over, not by a long shot. At 14:49, Tchaikovsky throws death to the floor. It surges faintly but at 15:06 is utterly vanquished. F-sharp is the last note we hear—the death rattle, perhaps, of death.

A spiritual revivification process begins at 15:09, as an extremely quiet F-sharp—once death's handmaiden—begins to throb. Tchaikovsky modulates to B major, which for a work in B minor is a startling and positive development. What happens next, in light of the preceding minutes, is miraculous: in a newly minted home key, Tchaikovsky once again rehearses life in its entirety. Beneath it, chromatic upsurges—the opposite of the chromatic death descent—pull the harmonies to surprising places, a groundswell of positive momentum. Now life gathers impetus, ameliorating all the unpleasantness of the preceding period when death seemed to have an icy grip. Flush and awash, at 16:24 Tchaikovsky lingers for a moment, ruminatively extemporizing on life on the pedal point of B—this could well be the coda, the end, a victory. Even the clarinet's solo aria at 16:46, answered as it is by tonic rolls on the timpani, is now recast as a final hopeful glance where before, in a different context, it sounded a song of loss. At 17:40, Tchaikovsky does something wonderfully strange, introducing a hopeful anthem based on the opening adagio material. By the second iteration of this material, at 17:52, there is a dissonance, a "blue" note. It resolves quickly, but this fly in the ointment, not repeated, is a dark portent, another twist of the knife—so that, as the music recedes, seemingly into victory, there is this one little persistent problem. He does not repeat it, but your ears have been set just wrong enough to wonder. We were wrecked, we made it through; we suffered and were redeemed; but foreboding times lie yet ahead in the great halls of the Tchaikovsky-verse. Do not get too comfortable. This victory is only temporary.

II. Allegro con grazia

The Tchaikovsky-verse is a peculiar place, equal parts straightforward and unearthly, elegant and absurd, genteel and phantasmagoric, bubbly and torturous. But even those most schooled in his antics could probably not, at the premiere of the "Pathetique" Symphony, have envisaged the bizarre turn that follows. If the opening section defied formal study—named themes suffice better than the more academic letters—this movement is infinitely more straightforward, cast in a typical rondo form—ABACABA—almost bland in its development, with one exception: it is in five. This is an irregular—and genuinely unprecedented—maneuver. It means that the rhythm—five beats to each measure as opposed to the more common three or four—will always seem uneasy, off, defiant of a tapping toe. It sounds, if you try to follow it closely, as if it bounces between a group of two beats and a group of three beats, a gorgeous asymmetry. Not since the Renaissance had a composer indulged in such rhythmic tomfoolery, such potent irony, writing a sweet, calm, lyrical section—almost a waltz—to which dancing would only end in tripped feet. The meter would not baffle a contemporary composer: after Stravinsky, who was prone to changing the meter every bar, a lilting 5/4 is hardly a dip into future shock. But for Tchaikovsky's set, this was positively outrageous—an affront or a thrill, depending on whom you asked. Even Wagner in his most "artwork of the future" mode would probably have stumbled trying to reckon this section. What makes the meter doubly hard to countenance is that the theme feels perfectly normal. Were you not told, you might listen to the entire movement unaware something peculiar was afoot. You might even presume that this was a waltz, as lovely and decorous as anything, but in the pit of your stomach, at the back of your mind, something would trouble you throughout. The movement would remain something you could almost follow, but ultimately a piece of music about which something was not at all right.

The material is certainly pretty, and commences without ceremony in the key of D major, the relative major to the home key of B minor (but in contrast to the B major ending of the preceding movement a piquant third away). The opening theme—theme A—first assayed in the cellos, climbs soulfully before plummeting downward. It is an elegant if obvious tune, built in four equal parts, melodic answer following melodic question. When Tchaikovsky passes it to the woodwinds, though it reads as slightly more expansive, nothing is really shocking or surprising. After the storms of the first movement, he wants to give us something a little less overt into which we can sink without trouble—but this remains the Tchaikovsky-verse, so his simplicity proves a fiendish sleight of hand. When theme A is repeated, it is absolutely unchanged save for the final measure, which the composer uses to step gently up into some new material—theme B.

This new theme is in the key of A major, the dominant of D major, and a conventional positioning for a second theme. Nothing out of ken here: Tchaikovsky is following all the rules, which, when set against the odd metric shenanigans, give his quirky choice greater impact. The material is a textbook second theme, a direct result of the first: where theme A moves up, theme B moves down, responding in kind with an answer to theme A's question. Quickly, Tchaikovsky commutes the theme from strings to woodwinds again, another perfect symmetry. It seems as if he is going to great lengths not to shock or dazzle, yet by doing so creating an even more chilling effect. When he sets motoric pizzicato strings against a return to theme A—a common trick the composer uses to activate his repeated themes—this too is somewhat rank-and-file predictable. It is not until a minute or so later that Tchaikovsky makes one of his signature moves, slipping down two half-steps, making the music more expansive, reaching to the bottom of the low strings while the violins hit their highest note yet, an effect tantamount to casting sunlight on an already beautiful meadow of flowers. A few seconds later, he is really soaring, using high strings to push the emotional envelope, while the horn, an inner voice, plays the melody. It is very touching, but in true Tchaikovsky fashion the whole to-do comes to a too smartly clipped close, as if to say, "So what?"

Tchaikovsky then introduces a heavy, Slavic lament in the movement's home key of D major—theme C—torturously sorrowful and pendulous. The odd meter causes it to feel even heavier, stretched and kneaded into long, lugubrious phrases. Feet fall heavier here, and it feels as if Tchaikovsky has been building to this overt wailing throughout, as if the lyricism of the first two themes were a mere subterfuge masking the latent underlying—overarching?—sorrow. To make the point, Tchaikovsky spreads theme C into three parts, a form (called a binary form) within a larger form, each of which repeats directly. He does not depart for some time, when, eventually, a shadow version of theme A is played in the woodwinds, while the strings carry on with what seems a third version of theme C. The shadow theme evolves, is traded between winds and strings, and ultimately wends its way (through the back door) to a repeat of theme A. But there is little satisfaction to this arrival, as it has been overprepared and sneaks beneath our radar—satisfaction being achieved mostly through the accumulation of expectations. Tchaikovsky wants you to experience the rediscovery of the opening material in an unsettling, creepy fashion, a furtive awakening from a dream rather than a triumph. Once you wake, you find yourself in exactly the same place, a direct repeat of theme A. When theme B returns, it too is largely unchanged, some slight tweaking of the scoring aside.

Tchaikovsky then redeploys his first repeat of theme A, the one activated by the pizzicato strings, and from here until the coda there is not a whiff of new material—but by this point you would be so aurally befuddled by what never seems to add up rhythmically. To be simultaneously both this conventional and this absurd is a glorious risk, one that Tchaikovsky takes headlong. And when we hear new material at the beginning of the coda, it is like an elegantly plotted raspberry. Tchaikovsky simply outlines the meter, one ascending note per beat, letting us know, in the last minute, the trickery he has been up to all along—less a punch-line than a condescending let-in on a joke you might not have gotten. This suffices until the moment when he glances once again at the sadness of theme C, lest we, amid his rhythmic chicanery, forget that this is a symphony of despair. When he touches on theme A one final time, it now feels desiccated, rent from grace—while above it, a lone clarinet, in its lowest, saddest register, plays a hollowed-out version of theme C. The end of the movement feels more like the final smothering of dying embers than a proper cadence.

III. Allegro molto vivace

Just when you thought things could not get any stranger in the Tchaikovsky-verse. the composer pulls a strange rabbit out of an even stranger hat. This movement is a scherzo (a mad dance most often in triple meter) that is twisted violently into a march rooted entirely in the repetition of a single, jaunty theme. It is ebullient, overtly joyful, so teeming with vitality as to be suspect. The question it broaches for the listener—which will remain long after the movement is complete—is whether the bluster of the movement is sincere or a brash nine-and-a-half minutes of smile-through-gritted-teeth suffused with the most flagrant, preposterous irony, out-Shostakovich-ing Shostakovich half a century before that composer made his terrifying faux-nationalist marches to appease the Soviet regime. The facts tell us that this is the music of a composer on the brink of suicide; the music tells a different story. Is he trying to hold his head up high, or is this some kind of manic cry, or is it a brazen march to the scaffold?

The movement begins with a scamper, an Allegro molto vivace (fast, very lively): a bouncy triple-meter figure in the strings reminiscent of the pellucid scuttling of Mendelssohn's "Queen Mab" Scherzo. Soaring wind and string cascades, all of which fly by at a lightning clip—and then repeat in case you blinked and missed them—follow three quick bars of this figuration. By shoving so many events into such a small space, Tchaikovsky prepares us for a cabinet-of-curiosities-style thrill ride. The first time we hear the melody—theme A—it is assigned to the oboes. Listen carefully because the bulk of this movement is made from this snappy little scrap.

Tchaikovsky quickly begins to develop the theme, though now there is a new flavor, in a harmony called the *Lydian* mode, which is like a major scale with a slight discoloration, a raised fourth degree. You do not need to understand the theory behind this, but you will probably be able to tell that there has been some sort of mild change in musical character: this is what lends the new development its dark-hued piquancy. Shortly thereafter, Tchaikovsky not only quickly departs from this new mode, but from the theme as well. He instead develops the accompaniment figure as a rollicking upward tradeoff between the different orchestral choirs of winds, brass, and strings. Less than a minute in, a new theme—theme B—is introduced (not so much theme as transition, but for convenience it can be labeled as such). This new tune employs the tension-generating device of two-against-three, or duple-against-triple, some parts being in 12/8, others in 4/4. Tchaikovsky soon returns to the introductory scampers and cascades, connecting directly to a more fleshed-out, grandiloquent theme B—a portent of the bombast to come.

Tchaikovsky then repeats theme B while a long held note in the bass helps to thicken the texture—as well as the plot: that note is our old friend F-sharp, the handmaiden of death, rearing its subliminal head. Almost is if to taunt it—and us in the process—Tchaikovsky lays on wild swoops of washing figuration (a stunning turn of orchestration) followed by a threatening storm flavored by careful iterations of theme A. The forward motion culminates in a severe orchestral hit, which in turn leads to a restatement of theme A in the clarinets. It sounds, in this scoring, like the background music for an energetic 1940s flyboy agitprop picture, hollow and yet somehow assured. What is also different about this repeat is that Tchaikovsky has changed the key to A major, a full step higher than the tonic, an unconventional but persuasive modulation. After theme A repeats twice, slightly swelled for the second iteration, the composer imposes an unadorned fanfare, a bold rhetorical sweep from the horns, beneath which a chromatic bass line descends—toying with, but not quoting, the same descent at the beginning of the entire symphony, the contract symbol for death. What the fanfare really does is split the mood off from the wiles of theme A so that a new motive—theme C—can be added.

This new theme is predicated on an intense, middle-register upward chromatic push—life struggling over the downward swell of death?—which contrasts both themes A and B. Like an annoying little "attaboy," theme A then returns, without ceremony, brimming with forced (ironic?) enthusiasm. From here, Tchaikovsky sinks deep into the enjoyment of his material, toying with it, chopping it up, and reassigning bits throughout the orchestra, gluing his patchwork together by the occasional mad cascade. It is not until a few minutes later, a long time in musical terms, that he substantially changes the texture, retreating both to his opening triple-meter pattern and the original key of G major. An exact repeat of the opening music—both themes A and B—ensues with very little changed (except some chiaroscuro shading through mildly altered orchestration).

The pulling back Tchaikovsky accomplishes follows a push of the material, spinning it out to what, in the hands of a less subtle composer, would have been an explosion. Tchaikovsky is crafty, makes us wait rather than give us the huge crash we expect. A single timpani rolls instead, quietly at first but building, until above it the theme is passed throughout the orchestra, creating a buildup of theme-A-related tension—a rousing speech given by a general the night before battle. The sheer exuberance of the music masks its deeper emotional lure: this is the sound of forced courage in the face of terror. The call to action reaches a near-erotic fevered pitch; eventually it explodes, shattering into wild, seething runs—among the most electrifying orchestral moments in Tchaikovsky's entire oeuvre.

For over ten terrifying seconds we are in no key, no section of the form, no harmony, no melody, the regularity of the soaring filigree the only thing that separates us from pure chaos. However, in the Tchaikovsky-verse what goes up will always come down, so theme A lands on its feet, almost as if the disturbed wailing of the previous measures never occurred. This rescue feels more manic than heroic, more echolalia than familiar friend, too familiar terra incognita. This is a military march coming apart at the seams—the huge crash that transpires does not inspire but sounds deafening and yet somehow furtive; it doth assent too much.

Theme C returns, unchanged except that now it is in the home key of G major. It seems as if Tchaikovsky is bringing this movement—more appropriate for Independence Day fireworks than the *1812* Overture—to a crashing close, hammering away not only at the themes but the tonic. The timpani roll clinches it—we are rounding in for what promises to be a loud cessation. Vivid, pounding chords (with dense horns filling in the middle, making them sound both bright and thick) push us endward, culminating in an ear-splitting texture (marked quadruple *forte*.). From here to the end, the coda is a minute of music Tchaikovsky would have us enjoy for its gusto and moxie. Dance now, he seems to say, for there's grieving yet to be done.

IV. Finale: Adagio lamentoso—Andante
CD 2, Track 5

This final movement of Tchaikovsky's last work is one of the most despairing musical essays ever written. Even the last pages of Mahler's death-drenched final symphony—with its depiction of a heart that struggles for life and loses—cannot compete with the desperate devastation that this final lamentation outlines. This is the last outpost of the Tchaikovsky-verse and its very finality stings, cuts us down, with a force of utter resignation too heavy to bear after the wild odyssey of the first three movements, which touched on the fear of death, the odd menace of death, and the grit and determination it takes to look death in the face. It is a struggle for life, a struggle in which the composer (and consequently the listener) is not victorious.

When the note of F-sharp—death's handmaiden in previous movements—played a role, it was always a cameo; in this movement, that note is the star, a grim wraith. Listen to the very beginning: there is a lyrical, descending theme in the strings—theme A—penitent before a tone in the winds that annoys the texture, disturbs the melody—the F-sharp. Try though the strings do, they cannot escape it. Even when it evolves into a countermelody, the note is still present in our mind's ear long after it is no longer being played . . . and it will, inevitably, return. In this movement, what tries to go up, like the strings which peak at 0:52, is taken down again—Tchaikovsky employs the winds, picking up where the strings left off, to gently move downward. Though he plays at a gathering of strength at 1:21, it is almost as if the strings get sucked back into the opening melody—the first note of which is F-sharp. A thinned repetition of the opening gesture follows, though instead of an attempt to soar, Tchaikovsky leads us, with great resignation, even further into the bottommost muck—from 2:20, asthmatic bassoons (remember the very opening of the piece?) ferry us to the depths.

Tchaikovsky introduces a new texture at 2:46: ululating horns, forming a thick rug on which a new theme—theme B—is presented. This new theme, also introduced in the strings, comes off as slightly more sanguine, prettier, though it too moves in a downward direction. It is short and simple, a scrap really, during which Tchaikovsky tries to make the same break for the skies that he did in theme A. At 4:38, the plea reaches an intoxicating flashpoint, but tumbles back to earth. This happens three times, though each time the first entreating note is lower than the last; the will is failing. As these questions were desperate, the smacking down is brutal, and in a vicious outburst, Tchaikovsky shoots us to the bottom with an incisive jolt at 4:53. This only instigates another iteration of theme B at 4:58, its efforts redoubled. There might be hope after all.

Alas, theme B, once so strong, begins to break down, supplicating at 5:30 to theme A—and its attendant F-sharp. Whatever we try, however much we beg, plead, sing, or cry, death awaits us. At 6:53, there is another glimmer of hope as theme A once again seeks redemption, climbing high, presumably to be shot down yet again. There is some triumph when, at 7:12, a climax—albeit a dark climax—is achieved. This one has potential, bent on taking us back to the light. But at 7:32, whatever brief hope we had is quashed by theme A—starting on an F-sharp, now favored by an F-sharp pedal in the bass, given a shiver by the F-sharp in the horns—we have little choice but to buckle and embrace the coming bleak inevitable.

The brass chorale at 8:09 is the dank music of pure resignation. The instruments struggle to rise above the F-sharp at the heart of their music, but they cannot win. At 8:53 there is one final stab at hope in the form of theme B, but it, like theme A before it, breaks down. The final note for which this iteration longs is F-sharp. Below the tune, we hear the descending chromatic. Death is quietly swirling all about us; it can no longer be denied or fought. And this theme, with its descent, will be the end of it all, moving inexorably downward as we struggle for air, gasp, and eventually—to the sound of a low chord played in the basses and cellos alone—pass from this world. The work began with the low strings, and that is how it ends. Ashes to ashes . . .

Notes

Chapter One

9 "My overture is getting on quite quickly": Quoted in Orlova, 1990, p. 23.

10 "You can tear it to pieces": Quoted in Orlova, 1990, p. 23.

10 "How very inspirational it is!": Quoted in Poznansky, 1991, p. 119.

10 "It is the best work": Quoted in Orlova, 1990, p. 24.

Chapter Two

19 "There was much applause": Quoted in Poznansky, p. 268.

19 "the pure creation of an artful master": Quoted in Poznansky, p. 269.

20 "Fateful force": Quoted in Poznansky, p. 269.

Chapter Three

37 "Only now": Quoted in Orlova, 1990, p. 114.

37 "I can imagine": Quoted in Brown, 1982, p. 264.

37 "I am very busy": Quoted in Orlova, 1990, p. 115.

38 "gave him great pleasure": Quoted in Brown, p. 260.

38 "The concerto is moving": Quoted in Orlova, 1990, p. 115.

38 "The first movement of the violin concerto": Quoted in Orlova, 1990, p. 116.

39 "It has been my dream": Quoted in Abraham, ii.

Chapter Four

54 "I don't think the piece has any serious merits": Quoted in Holden, 1995, p. 204.

54 "Krouglikov": Quoted in Holden, 1995, p. 205.

Chapter Five

59 "My muse": Quoted in Orlova, 1990, p. 210.

59 "To my surprise": Quoted in Orlova, 1990, p. 211.

59 "I have started to write again": Quoted in Poznansky, p. 380.

60 "It seems to me": Quoted in Garden, 1973, p. 97.

60 "At the moment": Quoted in Orlova, 1990, p. 264.

Chapter Six

77 "Now dear Madame": Quoted in Orlova, 1990, p. 386

93 "I am prouder": Quoted in Garden, 1973, p. 141.

94 "There will still be much that is new": Quoted in Orlova, 1990, p. 400.

95 "While on my travels": Quoted in Garden 1973, p. 139.

95 "This program": Quoted in Poznansky, p. 576.

96 "I must confess": Quoted in Garden, 1973, p. 140.

Bibliography

Abraham, Gerald. Essay accompanying the score of *Concerto for Violin and Orchestra in D Major, Op. 35*, by Pyotr Ilyich Tchaikovsky. Ernst Eulenburg ed. London: Ernst Eulenburg Ltd.

Brown, David. 1978. *Tchaikovsky: The Early Years 1840–1874*. New York: Norton.

————. 1982. *Tchaikovsky: The Crisis Years 1874–1878*. New York: Norton.

————. 1986. *Tchaikovsky: The Years of Wandering 1878–1885*. New York: Norton.

————. 1991. *Tchaikovsky: The Final Years 1885–1893*. New York: Norton.

————. 1993. *Tchaikovsky Remembered*. London: Faber and Faber.

Garden, Edward. 1973. *Tchaikovsky*. New York: Octagon Books.

Holden, Anthony. 1995. *Tchaikovsky: A Biography*. New York: Random House.

Orlova, Alexandra, comp. 1990. *Tchaikovsky: A Self-Portrait*. Trans. R. M. Davison. New York: Oxford University Press.

Poznansky, Alexander. 1991. *Tchaikovksy: The Quest for the Inner Man*. New York: Schirmer Books.

————. 1999. *Tchaikovsky Through Others' Eyes*. Bloomington: Indiana University Press.

CD Track Listing

CD 1

1. *Romeo and Juliet*: "Fantasy Overture" (19:18)
   Naxos 8.225931

2. *1812* Overture, Op. 49 (15:34)
   Naxos 8.225931

3. Serenade for Strings in C Major, Op. 48: I. (9:33)
   Naxos 8.554048

4. *Nutcracker*: "Miniature Overture" (3:24)

5. *Nutcracker*: "Marche" (2:23)

6. *Nutcracker*: "Danse de la Fée-Dragée" ("Dance of the Sugar Plum Fairies") (1:49)

7. *Nutcracker*: "Danse Russe Trépak" ("Russian Dance: Trépak") (1:11)

8. *Nutcracker*: "Danse Arabe" ("Arabian Dance") (2:56)

9. *Nutcracker*: "Danse Chinoise" ("Chinese Dance") (1:14)

10. *Nutcracker*: "Danse des Mirlitons" ("Dance of the Red Pipes") (2:24)

11. *Nutcracker*: "Valse des Fleurs" ("Waltz of the Flowers") (6:54)
    Naxos 8.553271

CD 2

1. Symphony No. 4: I. Andante sostenuto—Moderato con anima (19:00)

2. Symphony No. 4: IV. Finale: Allegro con fuoco (9:16)
   Naxos 8.550488

3. Concerto for Violin: I. Allegro moderato (20:02)
   Naxos 8.550124

4. Symphony No. 6 in B minor, Op. 74: I. Adagio—Allegro non troppo (18:55)

5. Symphony No. 6 in B minor, Op. 74: IV. Finale: Adagio lamentoso—Andante (10:49)
   Naxos 8.550782